# Legacies

## A practical guide for charities

*edited by*
Michael Norton

A Directory of Social Change Publication

LEGACIES: A PRACTICAL GUIDE FOR CHARITIES

Edited and designed by Michael Norton
Cover design by Ruth Lowe

First published 1983

The Directory of Social Change, 9 Mansfield Place, London NW3 1HS

ISBN 0 907164 11 0

Photoset by Scarborough Typesetting Services, Scarborough, N. Yorkshire
Printed and bound in Great Britain by Biddles of Guildford

*British Library Cataloguing in Publication Data*

Norton, Michael
    Legacies.
    1. Fund raising—Handbooks, manuals, etc.
    I. Title
    361.7'3'0942        HV41

    ISBN 0–907164–11–0

# Contents

# Acknowledgements

The editor acknowledges the help given in compiling this book from the following people: Anthony Clay of RSPB, Asher Corren of Nightingale House and Philip Mellor of Westmore Advertising whose presentations at a Seminar on 'Raising Money Through Legacies' have formed the basis of the section on how to increase your legacy income; Richard Wells of Lloyds Bank Trust Division and Ken Bryon and Brian Miles of the RNLI for their help in producing the section of the book on the legal aspects of legacy giving; Mr. D. J. F. Ford of Smee and Ford for supplying information for the Appendix on the notification service his company provides; and the staff of the Capital Taxes Office of the Inland Revenue for commenting on the Appendix on Capital Transfer Tax.

# Introduction

Legacies can be an important source of income for a charity. They represent as much as 10 per cent of the total income that all charities receive; and one third of the total amount given by individuals to charity each year is given in the form of legacies.

Many of the large charities have geared themselves up to get legacy income, and they do this with a great measure of success. Many other charities ignore this source of income – either because they have not got round to doing anything yet, or because they do not know what to do, or perhaps because they have considered it and rejected the possibility as being inappropriate to them.

Many of the charities who do not get any legacy income at all could probably get some; and often this can be done with very little effort. And those that are getting some legacy income might be able to get a great deal more. One problem has been the lack of information or advice on what charities can do to increase their legacy income.

This book is a practical guide which covers all aspects of getting legacy income. It starts by looking at the importance of legacy income to charities, at the size of the legacy cake and at who is getting what. It shows you how a charity can advertise for legacy income and then goes on to give some simple and practical advice on how to set about increasing the amount of legacy income that your charity is getting. It also considers the memorial aspect of donations; this is a separate but related way in which a charity can raise money. It looks at the problems that can occur in the drafting of Wills and in their administration. And finally it looks at the taxation aspects of legacies and other gifts of capital to charity, and at the statutory provisions for families and dependants to inherit (someone may want to give all they have to charity, but they may not in practice be able to do so!).

1

# INTRODUCTION

This is the first practical guide to legacy income for charities. We hope that its advice will be invaluable, and that it will open up new areas of fund-raising for many charities.

Michael Norton
May 1983

# PART I

# THE IMPORTANCE OF LEGACIES

# A first step

Any charity can ask its supporters to remember them in their Will. This book fills in the details of how legacies work, the tax reliefs that are available and how charities can get more legacy income.

But if you want to get going without reading any further, then you should write to your supporters, asking them to leave you money in their Will. Here are some of the points you might make in such a letter:

1. **You should consider making a Will**, if you have not already done so. A Will directs how your estate will be distributed and assures that it is distributed as you would wish. Making a Will will ensure that those who you wish to provide for are provided for; you can also take into account tax considerations so that you and your family minimise your tax burden; and you ensure that the administration of your affairs when you die is handled smoothly at what will inevitably be a difficult time for those who survive you. When you make your Will please consider leaving us a legacy.

2. **We need the money:** we depend on donations from our supporters and the public. You have already shown your support for our work. We would now like to ask you to remember us in your Will. You don't have to be wealthy to leave us a legacy. Every little bit helps.

3. **You will be helping a worthwhile cause:** our work is important and our needs are pressing (state your case and state it powerfully).

4. **It costs you nothing:** we will get the money only when you have no further use for it. What better memorial could you hope for than to provide help for sick children, countryside protection, fighting cancer (or whatever). And there may be

tax advantages too. If your estate is liable to Capital Transfer Tax, then there will be less tax to pay if you make a charitable bequest.

5. **There are two main forms of legacy** which you might like to consider: a pecuniary legacy or a residuary legacy. A pecuniary legacy is a specific cash sum which you mention in your Will. A residuary legacy is the residue of your estate after all other legacies, debts, Capital Transfer Tax and expenses have been paid, or a share of the residue of your estate. You may also wish to consider a conditional bequest, bequeathing your estate to (say) your wife, but if she dies before you then the estate will go to charity.

6. **A Will is a legal document.** If you want to alter an existing Will by adding a Codicil or if you wish to draw up a new Will, we would strongly advise you to seek professional advice from a solicitor (or from your bank). We suggest the following wording for a legacy:

**For a pecuniary legacy:**

I give to . . . . . (*state name, address and charity registration number of the charity*) . . . . . (hereinafter called 'the Charity') the sum of £. . . . . (*amount of the legacy*) . . . . . free of duty, such sum to be applied to the general purposes of the Charity towards the promotion of its objects and I direct that a receipt of the Honorary Treasurer or other authorised officer for the time being of the Charity shall be a good and sufficient discharge to my Executors for the payment of the aforesaid legacy.

**For a residuary legacy:**

I give devise and bequeath all ( . . . . . *or a share of* . . . . . ) residue of my estate absolutely to the . . . . . (*state name, address and charity registration number of the charity*) . . . . . (hereinafter called 'the Charity'), such sum to be applied to the general purposes of the charity and I direct that a receipt of the Honorary Treasurer or other authorised officer for the time being of the Charity shall be a good and sufficient discharge to my Executors.

There are many different forms of wording that charities use. However, the wording for a charitable bequest should contain the following ingredients:

(a) A description of the legacy or sum bequeathed. This can be adapted for gifts in kind (but these should be clearly described to avoid complications).

(b) The details of the recipient charity described clearly and unambiguously.

(c) A statement that the sum be applied to certain purposes. This will normally be for the general purposes of the charity. It might also state that the sum may be used by the charity either as income or as capital. Or it might specify that the sum be applied for a particular charitable purpose (to the West Front appeal or clock tower restoration fund, or to add to the charity's permanent endowment).

(d) A discharge clause which relieves the Executors of any responsibility for seeing that the money is spent properly. A receipt for the legacy from an authorised officer of the charity discharges the Executors from any further responsibility once the money is paid over.

The suggested wording given here will suit donors and charities in most circumstances. If you wish to have a more complicated form of wording containing conditions specific to the requirements of your charity, then it is advisable to take legal advice on the form of the wording you are recommending to your supporters.

7. **You can add a Codicil to your existing Will**, if you have already made a Will and would now like to support us. You don't have to make a new Will. We suggest the following form of wording for a Codicil:

### Codicil

*Please complete this form and place it with your Will (but do not attach it to your Will):*

I . . . . . . . . . . . . . . . . . .*(name)*. . . . . . . . . . . . . . . . . . of
. . . . . . . . . . . . . . . .*(address)*. . . . . . . . . . . . . . . . declare
this to be a first *(or second, etc. . . )* Codicil which I make this
. . . . .*(date)*. . . . . day of . . . . .*(month)*. . . . . one thousand
nine hundred and . . . . .*(year)*. . . . . to my Will which is

dated the .....(date)..... day of .....(month).....
one thousand nine hundred and .....(year).....

I give and bequeath to the ......(name of charity)......
of ...................(address)...................
Charity Registration No. ......(number)..... the sum of
£ .....(amount of legacy)..... free of duty for the general
purposes of the Charity and I direct that a receipt of the
Honorary Treasurer or other authorised officer for the
time being of the Charity shall be a good and sufficient
discharge to my Executors for the payment of the aforesaid legacy.

In Witness whereof I have hereunto set my hand this day

Signed by the above-named

........ (name) ........
as a Codicil to his(her)          Signed:
Will in our joint presence
and then by us in his(hers):

Witnessed by ...........   Witnessed by ...........
Name.................   Name.................
Occupation .............   Occupation .............
Address ...............   Address ...............

The next step is to compose a letter – in the most persuasive
terms, of course – encouraging your supporters to leave you a
legacy.

# Legacy income: some facts and figures

This section will examine the importance of legacy income to charities. Many charities, particularly smaller charities, under-estimate the importance of legacy income as a possible source of money for their work. Through an analysis of the published figures for charity giving overall and an examination of the accounts of some of the larger charities, it can be demonstrated that legacies do present an opportunity for a wide spectrum of charities to raise money.

Obviously the largest sums go to the larger nationally known charities. But smaller charities can be equally successful, relative to their size, in getting legacy income, and the figures clearly demonstrate this. So the notion that *'legacy income is not for us, but only for the big boys'* cannot be justified.

Some causes are particularly successful in attracting legacies, whilst others do fare rather less well. But even if you think that your cause is not as attractive as some other causes, you should still think carefully about the possibilities of legacy income; and you should certainly approach your committed supporters and ask them to leave you money in their Will.

To elaborate on these broad conclusions, let us examine the facts and figures of legacy giving.

## 1. Legacies are important

Let us start by looking at how important legacies are as a source of income for charities in Britain today.

9

# LEGACY INCOME: SOME FACTS AND FIGURES

**For 1980–81 the income of charities was estimated as being:**

| | | £ million |
|---|---|---|
| **Donated income** | Lifetime gifts from individuals | 496 |
| | Legacies and bequests | 260 |
| | Company donations | 50 |
| | Grant-making trusts | 258 |
| **Government support** | Central government grants | 124 |
| | Local government grants | 120 |
| **Earned income** | Trading | 129 |
| | Lotteries | 11 |
| | Fees and charges for services, etc. | 430 |
| **Unearned income** | Investment income, rents, etc. | 765 |
| **Total income** | | 2643 |

*(These figures are compiled by the Charities Aid Foundation. They are derived from various sources. Some are based on reasonably accurate data whilst others are no more than inspired guesses. But they are the best figures available at the moment, and they do give a reasonable indication of where charities actually get their money from, even if they are not wholly accurate.)*

Looking at these figures we can draw a number of conclusions:

(a) **Legacy income is important.** Legacies represent almost exactly 10 per cent of the total income of charities. Obviously not all charities are equally successful in attracting legacy income. But we will show that legacy income is an important source of income for many smaller charities as well as for the big national charities.

(b) **Legacy income is more important than some other sources of income that charities obtain.** Many charities turn to industry instinctively when looking for money. Yet industry gives only one fifth of what charities get in the form of legacies each year. Some other charities see trusts

10

and government as their most likely source of funding. Yet legacies represent an equally important source of funds as the grants that can be obtained from grant-making trusts. And individuals give as much when they die as central and local government put together.

(c) **Individuals are predisposed to leave money to charity when they die.** One third of the amount given to charity by individuals each year is given in the form of legacies. The other two thirds is given in the form of lifetime gifts (and this includes the whole spectrum of donations, covenants, street collections, membership subscriptions, sponsored walks, fund-raising events, and so on).

Not everyone gives money to charity during their lifetime, and not everyone leaves money to charity in their Will. But **on average a legacy is likely to be twenty-five times the size of a lifetime gift**. This fact can be demonstrated by making the following approximate calculation: Assuming that people live to seventy and that they give to charity over their adult life, then approximately one fiftieth of the adult population will die each year. So in any year there are fifty times as many people who could make a lifetime gift as there are people who could make a bequest to charity. The amount given in the form of lifetime gifts is almost exactly double that given in the form of legacies. So the average legacy will be twenty-five times as large as the average amount given by an individual to charity each year during his lifetime. These are crude figures, but they give us an 'order of magnitude' for comparing the size of legacies with lifetime giving.

So we have demonstrated that legacies represent a large source of income for charities and that the amount given to charity by someone on death is likely to be very substantially greater than the value of a lifetime gift from the same person.

## 2. Legacy income is important for all charities

In 1980–81 the legacy cake amounted to £260 million. This was divided up as follows:

**Top 25 charities\*** obtained £75.9 million in legacies, or 29% of all legacy income

# LEGACY INCOME: SOME FACTS AND FIGURES

**Top 50 charities\*** obtained £91.5 million in legacies, or 35% of all legacy income

**Top 200 charities** obtained £107 million in legacies, or 41% of all legacy income

---

**All other charities** obtained £153 million in legacies, or 59% of all legacy income

\* *Charities ranked in order of their success in obtaining legacy income*
*The top 25 all obtained over £1 million in legacies*
*The top 50 all obtained over £425,000 in legacies*

The big charities are much more successful in attracting legacy income than the smaller charities, as is to be expected. The average legacy income is as follows:

| | |
|---|---|
| **Top 25 charities** | £3 million per annum |
| **Top 200 charities** | £530,000 per annum |
| **All other charities** | £1,200 per annum |

But the big charities are also much more successful in attracting other forms of income. In fact the reported legacy income for the top 200 charities is almost exactly the same proportion of the total income received in the form of donations from individuals as for all charities:

**For the top 200 charities:**
Legacy income £107 million
Lifetime gifts £222 million
Legacies represent 33% of the total gifts from individuals

**For all other charities:**
Legacies £153 million
Lifetime gifts £276 million
Legacies represent 35½% of the total gifts from individuals

So legacy income is obtained by all charities and not just by the large charities. In fact after allowing for their size, the **smaller** charities appear to be equally successful in attracting legacy income as the larger charities. This is an extremely important point. It contradicts the notion that legacy income is for the larger seemingly more successful charities only, which may be a major reason why many smaller charities do not actively seek legacy income.

3. **Legacy income has been a growing source of income in recent years**

For all charities *(£ million)*

|  | Legacy income | Trust income | Company donations | Government grants |
|---|---|---|---|---|
| **1980–81** | 260 | 258 | 50 | 244 |
| **1979–80** | 205 | 219 | 44 | 242 |
| **1978–79** | 190 | 195 | 43 | 220 |
| **1977–78** | 165 | 170 | 42 | 200 |

During the period 1977–81 inflation reached nearly 25% per annum. So to get a better view of how legacy income has grown in real terms, we need to adjust these figures for the rises that have occurred in the Retail Prices Index.

For all charities *(1980–81 = 100)*

|  | Legacy income | Trust income | Company donations | Government grants |
|---|---|---|---|---|
| **1980–81** | 100 | 100 | 100 | 100 |
| **1979–80** | 90.8 | 97.7 | 101.6 | 114.1 |
| **1978–79** | 98.6 | 102.0 | 116.6 | 121.7 |
| **1977–78** | 86.5 | 96.4 | 123.2 | 119.9 |

These figures show that legacy income has grown rather faster than the rate of inflation, increasing steadily and by nearly one sixth over the last five years. During the same period trust income has remained fairly stable, whereas the income received in the form of company donations and government grants has shown a marked decline.

Different factors affect the levels of these different sources of income from year to year. Government grants at central government and local government levels have been affected by the squeeze on public expenditure. Company donations have been affected by the fall in company profitability, and possibly also by the emergence of sponsorship, which is treated as a business expense and is not included in these figures. Sponsorship is largely confined to sports and the arts as a method of giving (the amount given in sponsorship is reckoned to be about equal to the amount given as charitable donations, but most sponsorship money goes to a few highly televised sports and to the major national cultural institutions). Trust income is mainly affected by the growth in investment income, which includes dividends on shareholdings, rents on property and interest on other forms of investments. Legacy income is affected to a very great extent by the level of house prices and by the level of share prices. Real estate and investments in stocks and shares are the two major ingredients of any estate; so where a charity is bequeathed a share of the residue of an estate (a residual legacy) rather than a fixed amount (a pecuniary legacy), the amount of the estate will be considerably affected by the prevailing levels of share prices and of property prices.

Next let us look at the growth in legacy income for the top 200 charities. The figures that are available are derived from the reported annual income as stated in the charity's accounts. Over the same five year period, the reported legacy income of the top 200 charities has grown rather faster than the total legacy cake:

**Top 200 charities reported legacy income** *(£ million)*

|         | Legacy income | Lifetime gifts |      |
|---------|---------------|----------------|------|
| 1980–81 | 107           | 222            | 33%  |
| 1979–80 | 92            | 201            | 31%  |
| 1978–79 | 66            | 162            | 29%  |
| 1977–78 | 52            | 120            | 30%  |

The reasons for this may be: (a) better reporting by charities in recent years so that more and more charities are now identifying legacies as a stated source of income in their published accounts; and (b) the figures for all charities are an informed guess rather than based on reported information.

Allowing for the fact that legacy income is now better reported, it does seem to have very roughly represented a constant proportion of the total giving by individuals to charity.

**4. Which types of charity are the most successful in attracting legacy income**

In 1981–82, 116 charities received over £100,000 in legacy income. Analysing these into various categories of charitable activity, the following picture emerges:

| | Total legacy income by category *(£ million)* | % of total | No. of charities in category |
|---|---|---|---|
| **Cancer** | 24.1 | 24 | 10 |
| **Disability** | 15.3 | 15 | 18 |
| **Relief of distress** | 15.3 | 15 | 29 |
| **Animal welfare** | 12.5 | 12 | 13 |
| **Children** | 11.6 | 11 | 7 |
| **Medical** | 7.5 | 7 | 18 |
| **Lifeboats** | 5.8 | 6 | 1 |
| **Overseas aid and relief** | 4.4 | 4 | 6 |
| **Religion** | 3.6 | 3 | 11 |
| **Heritage and conservation** | 2.6 | 3 | 3 |
| **Total for top 116 charities** | 102.7 | 100 | 116 |

Looking at these figures, the first impression is that legacy income is fairly well spread over the whole range of charitable activity.

The particular success of cancer charities and animal charities in attracting legacy income should be noted. Cancer is said to be the single most emotive word in attracting legacies, and any charity operating for the benefit of animals can also count itself particularly fortunate when seeking legacies. One point to note is that no arts or recreational organisation obtains enough legacy income to be included in this list. And as might be expected, the top 116 charities consist almost entirely of 'national' charities. Another important factor is the success of particular individual charities in attracting legacy income. Three-quarters of the legacies to cancer charities is obtained by two charities, the Cancer Research Campaign and The Imperial Cancer Research Fund, who between them received a staggering £18.2 million in 1980–81. Over half the legacies to children's charities were obtained by one charity, Dr. Barnardo's, which received £6.0 million in 1980–81. And the lifeboat category consists entirely of legacies to the Royal National Lifeboat Institution.

When people leave money to charity they are either supporting a particular charity that they wish to support, or they are supporting a particular area of charitable activity that they wish to support. The spread of legacy income probably reflects the concerns and cares of people leaving money to charity. It should be remembered that they do not represent an average cross-section of the community, but they consist very largely of older people and the better off (who have more money to give away). They may also be largely female – as women tend to live longer and marry earlier, and so may be more likely to have no immediate dependents to leave their money to. The success of particular charities in attracting legacy income depends on how well they are able to attract public support. It also depends on how successful they are in promoting a particular cause as being urgent, and on how well they project themselves as being the charity that comes to mind when people think of that cause (e.g.: children, old people, the blind, dumb animals, the destitute, etc.).

## 5. Who gets legacy income

### (a) The large charities

First let us look at the larger charities:

The top 20 charities for legacy income (as reported) for 1981–82 were:

16

# LEGACY INCOME: SOME FACTS AND FIGURES

| | Total voluntary income (£m) | Total legacy income (£m) | Order of ranking for total voluntary income |
|---|---|---|---|
| Imperial Cancer Research Fund | 12.9 | 10.1 | 3 |
| Cancer Research Campaign | 12.7 | 8.1 | 2 |
| Dr. Barnardo's | 11.4 | 6.0 | 5 |
| Royal National Lifeboat Institution | 11.9 | 5.8 | 4 |
| Royal National Institute for the Blind | 7.6· | 5.1 | 12 |
| Royal Society for the Prevention of Cruelty to Animals | 5.1 | 4.8 | 17 |
| Salvation Army | 10.5 | 3.5 | 6 |
| People's Dispensary for Sick Animals | 4.5 | 3.3 | 21 |
| Guide Dogs for the Blind | 4.9 | 2.5 | 19 |
| British Heart Foundation | 4.8 | 2.5 | 20 |
| Arthritis and Rheumatism Council | 3.9 | 2.3 | 24 |
| Leonard Cheshire Foundation | 2.7 | 2.2 | 30 |
| Marie Curie Memorial Foundation | 5.6 | 2.0 | 14 |
| St. Dunstan's | 2.0 | 2.0 | 38 |
| National Society for the Prevention of Cruelty to Children | 5.4 | 1.8 | 15 |
| National Trust | 10.2 | 1.7 | 7 |
| Distressed Gentlefolk's Aid Association | 1.9 | 1.6 | 40 |
| Church of England Children's Society | 4.4 | 1.6 | 22 |
| British Red Cross Society | 8.4 | 1.5 | 9 |
| Spastics Society | 7.4 | 1.4 | 13 |

17

# LEGACY INCOME: SOME FACTS AND FIGURES

The top 20 charities ranked in order of their voluntary income (that is the income they raise in the form of donations) for 1981–82 were:

|  | Total voluntary income (£m) | Total legacy income (£m) | Order of ranking for legacy income |
|---|---|---|---|
| Oxfam | 13.3 | 1.2 | 21 |
| Cancer Research Campaign | 12.9 | 8.1 | 2 |
| Imperial Cancer Research Fund | 12.7 | 10.1 | 1 |
| Royal National Lifeboat Institution | 11.9 | 5.8 | 4 |
| Dr. Barnardo's | 11.4 | 6.0 | 3 |
| Salvation Army | 10.5 | 3.5 | 7 |
| National Trust | 10.2 | 1.7 | 16 |
| Save the Children Fund | 9.8 | 0.7 | 34 |
| British Red Cross | 8.4 | 1.5 | 19 |
| Help the Aged | 7.9 | * | * |
| Christian Aid | 8.1 | 0.6 | 40 |
| Royal National Institute for the Blind | 7.6 | 5.1 | 5 |
| Spastics Society | 7.4 | 1.4 | 20 |
| Marie Curie Memorial Foundation | 5.6 | 2.0 | 13 |
| National Society for the Prevention of Cruelty to Children | 5.4 | 1.8 | 15 |
| Royal British Legion | 5.3 | 0.4 | 55 |
| Royal Society for the Prevention of Cruelty to Animals | 5.1 | 4.8 | 6 |
| Action Aid | 5.0 | ** | ** |
| Guide Dogs for the Blind | 4.9 | 2.5 | 9 |
| British Heart Foundation | 4.8 | 2.5 | 10 |

\* *no figures are published for Help the Aged, but their legacy income is likely to be substantial.*

\*\* *Action Aid's legacy income is too low to appear in the rankings, amounting to only £24,000 in 1981–82.*

Comparing these two lists raises a number of questions:

Why does Dr. Barnardo's get nearly £6 million in legacy income, whereas Save the Children Fund only gets £¾ million?

Why do Action Aid and the Royal British Legion receive only minimal legacy income?

LEGACY INCOME: SOME FACTS AND FIGURES

Why is so much of the RSPCA's voluntary income received in the form of legacies?

Why do St. Dunstan's, the Leonard Cheshire Foundation and the Distressed Gentlefolk's Aid Association receive so much legacy income?

Why does Oxfam, the most successful of the fund-raising charities, raise relatively quite little in legacy income?

If you could find satisfactory answers to these questions, you should be well on the way to working out ways of increasing the legacy income of your charity. But before we delve any deeper, let us look at some more figures.

## (b) Charities who have done well and charities who have done badly

Amongst the top 200 charities there are some who have done particularly well and some who have done relatively rather badly:

| Legacy income (£,000) | 1977–78 | 1978–79 | 1979–80 | 1980–81 | 1981–82 |
|---|---|---|---|---|---|
| **Four high fliers** | | | | | |
| Salvation Army | 334 | 648 | 699 | 2996 | 3536 |
| British Heart Foundation | 601 | 1061 | 1055 | 1477 | 2531 |
| Arthritis and Rheumatism Council | 846 | 970 | 1290 | 1673 | 2371 |
| Royal Society for the Protection of Birds | 140 | 261 | 544 | 551 | 656 |
| **Some smaller charities that have not done quite so well:** | | | | | |
| Friends of the Elderly | 243 | 450 | 286 | 225 | 134 |
| Royal Hospital and Home for Incarables | 271 | 272 | 239 | 260 | 215 |
| Greater London Fund for the Blind | 160 | 194 | 128 | 145 | 135 |

The full extent of these figures is masked by the fact that the cost of living index rose by nearly two-thirds over the period in question.

This raises two more questions:

**Why do some charities do well?**

**Why do others do badly** *(in the legacy stakes)*?

19

Now let us see if we can find some answers to all these questions. These will be based largely on common sense, rather than on any scientifically determined facts – for all too little research has been done in the field of legacy income. But common sense, even if it does not provide us with the absolute truth, should at least point us in the right direction.

There are three main elements that we need to consider for a charity obtaining a legacy.

1. The donor, who makes a Will leaving money to the charity.

2. The charity, which will receive the money on the death of the donor.

3. The communication between the charity and the donor (and the public generally) of the importance of the cause and the need to support the charity.

Or, expressed in another way, the following are important:

**What you are:** The nature and suitability of your cause.

**Who you reach:** Who your supporters are and who your potential supporters might be.

**What you do:** How you make your appeal and how well you are able to influence your supporters.


## 6. How to get legacy income

In one sense trying to get legacy income is no different from trying to get people to give to charity in any other way. You must give your supporters (and others who might be predisposed to support you) the opportunity to remember you in their Will. You may want to go one step further than that and try to persuade them (discreetly, of course) to leave money to you. 'If you do not ask, you will not get'. This is the first and most important law of fund-raising. And it applies equally to legacies as to other forms of donation.

This gives you two target audiences:

(a) Your existing network of supporters. This includes members, friends, your local branch network, volunteer helpers, staff, the people for whom you provide charitable services and their families.

(b) The general public, amongst whom there might be a surprising number of people prepared to support you if only you could find a way of telling them about what you do and why you need money.

So if you do have supporters (and in particular well-heeled supporters) and if you do have a national (or local) presence and are generally known as being a worthy organisation, then this is a good start. For smaller charities, the self-confidence that you will continue to exist in the future is also important. If you struggle from year to year, or if you are entirely dependent on a local authority grant which may be cut at any time, you are probably too worried about the present to look to the long-term future. And it is difficult to persuade someone to leave money to you, if in your heart of hearts you believe that they will live longer than your organisation.

There is one important aspect in which legacy income is completely different from other sources of income. The average period between a last Will being made and the testator's death is approximately four years. This means that at the time when the decision is made to leave money to charity, the people making the decisions will very largely be the elderly. Of course younger people do make Wills, but they are likely to live on to make subsequent Wills, and they may then decide to change their charitable dispositions altogether. So it is the elderly who, by and large, will be deciding the distribution of legacy income. There is also the fact that women tend to marry earlier and live longer – so a husband is more likely to have a surviving spouse to leave his estate to than a wife, who is more likely to end up a widow.

How the elderly wish to dispose of their money will reflect their own particular concerns, which will probably not be the same as the most pressing needs in society. A Charity Commissioner in the 19th Century called Arthur Hobhouse railed against the establishment of grant-making trusts, calling them 'government from the grave'. A person could amass a fortune, and then tie this up in a charitable trust which would exist in perpetuity. His wishes (as reflected in the purpose of the trust) which might be mean-minded or which might be philanthropic, which might be totally eccentric or which might relate to the very pressing needs of the time, would dictate how the money should be spent **beyond his grave**.

Similarly a legacy might be defined as 'government at the graveside'. People making Wills are in the evening of their lives.

Their views about the current state of society are likely to be very different from society as a whole; for example;

Old ladies may see unemployed youths as potential muggers rather than as a deprived group at risk, which is deserving of support.

Old ladies (again) may be living alone and strike up the most important relationships with their pets or with the birds feeding on the windowsill, and a legacy to an animal charity is a means of saying 'thank you' to these creatures for their companionship.

Older people may see drug addicts or unsupported lone parents as entirely deserving of their situation, rather than as people with pressing needs.

Older people may have a view of society based on the situation as it existed thirty or fifty years ago; their attitudes may well be old-fashioned and they may not agree with 'new fangled notions' such as penal reform or animal liberation.

Older people will be concerned about disease and death, both because this is a direct concern for themselves and because their friends are dying. So charities concerned with cancer, heart disease, arthritis, rheumatism, failing sight, deafness, will be prominent on their lists of worthy charities.

Charities that look after the old will also find favour. Old people's homes, old people's housing charities, relief charities (including those that help people from their own class – Distressed Gentlefolk's Aid Association and Professional Classes Aid Society, etc.) are likely to be successful in getting legacies. These are the charities that have helped them or that have helped their friends.

So if you are a cancer charity or the Battersea Dogs Home or the Barking Cats Home, then you are off to a good start. Certain charities will find it very easy to raise money through legacies; others may find it well nigh impossible. It pays to think a little about where you stand in the popularity stakes before you start thinking about how to get legacy income.

It is not simply a matter of what you do, but also of who is involved in your work. Are you a charity which reflects the interests of the younger generation and which involves younger people in its work? If so you are less likely to get any substantial legacy income than if you attract older people as your supporters and helpers. And if you attract the better off, then that is also an added advantage! You will also need to understand a little about why people want to leave money to charity.

There are many reasons why people might wish to make a legacy to charity. Here are some common ones:

**Pagoda building.** Their place in heaven is determined by the number of pagodas they build during their life or the amount of good they do (or the amount they leave to charity on their death).

**The memorial aspect.** Death is the leveller, but their name can live on through a legacy. Smaller local charities may have the edge here as they have a greater opportunity to provide a living memorial than if the money is poured into the more anonymous coffers of, say, the large cancer charities.

**Life beyond the grave.** Death is the end of their life, but they can continue having influence beyond the grave by leaving their money for some charitable purpose.

**Cheating the taxman.** There are positive tax advantages in leaving money to charity.

**Spite.** To avoid giving the money to particular people; although certain people now have a right to inherit under the Family Inheritance Act; and even though a testator may cut them out of a Will, they may still be able to obtain a share of the estate.

**The done thing.** They feel they ought to leave at least something to charity. But in fact it is only a small minority of people who actually do so.

**Saying thank you for help** that they or their friends have received from a particular charity.

**A positive gesture**, because they wish to do something to solve a particular problem; perhaps they would like to have done something about it during their lives, but they never got around to doing so.

**A positive gesture** (again), because they wish to help a charity that they have been connected with as a volunteer, committee member, enthusiastic supporter, etc.

**The only option.** They have no living relatives or family, or none that they wish to benefit, and a charity seems a better bet than leaving their money to the government or the Crown.

If you begin to understand why people give, you will have a better idea of how to persuade them to give to you. You will also want to try to understand how they decide which particular charity to support. Again, there are several common reasons:

They have some existing or previous connection with the charity. You may not even be aware of this connection. But they may be on your supporters list; and then you will have the opportunity to reach them.

They may wish to give to you because they have heard about your work. Naturally good publicity and PR helps.

They may have responded to a specific public appeal.

They may wish to give to a particular type of charitable activity and your charity is the one that immediately springs to mind; here are some examples of this:

| | |
|---|---|
| Lifeboats | – RNLI |
| Animals | – RSPCA |
| Children | – Barnardo's or NSPCC |
| Cancer | – Imperial Cancer Research or Cancer Research Campaign |
| Old People | – Help the Aged |
| An obviously good cause | – The Salvation Army, etc. |

If this is the case, then it is important that people know about you. A large charity can mount a major advertising campaign as a way of achieving this; a smaller charity may have to think more creatively.

They may ask the advice of a solicitor when drawing up their Will; hence many charities advertise to solicitors.

Having thought a little about why people give and what they like to give to, you are now in a position to build on this and develop a strategy for getting legacy income for your charity. You will have to:

1. Persuade people to **give** to charity and to make charitable bequests.

24

2. Persuade those that do give to leave **more** to charity.

3. Persuade them to give **to your own charity**.

Although charities get £260 million in legacy income annually, this is only a small fraction of the total value of the assets of people dying in any one year. It represents only about £350 per person.

Most people leave nothing at all to charity. Smee and Ford, who provide a notification service to charities (*see Appendix 4*), estimate that of over 5,000 wills inspected each week at Somerset House only some 200 to 250 contain charitable bequests. This is only about 5 per cent of the total; and since some people do die intestate, the proportion of people leaving money to charity is still lower than this. As another indication of the relative unimportance of charitable bequests, in the Consumers' Association guide to making a Will charitable bequests are barely touched upon. But a few people do give very substantially and many more give something. Charities are not really competing against one another to get a larger share of the legacy cake. The main task for them is to persuade more people to give more to charity when they die, and thereby to increase the size of the legacy cake available to charities as a whole.

## 7. Two drawbacks of legacy income

If you do decide that your charity should be doing more to get legacy income, what then are the drawbacks?

### (a) Legacy income is not immediate income

To get legacy income you have to persuade people to make a Will (or to add a codicil to an existing Will) leaving money to your charity. They then have to die before you get any money, and it can then take a year or more of administration before you actually receive the cash.

There is an average period of around four years between the date when people make their last Will and when they die. Of course this does not mean that people will die four years after they have made a Will – this would be a big disincentive to making a Will at all! Many people will make more than one Will during their lives, and their expectation of life at the time they make their Will will depend on their age and their general health.

25

Many charities aim their legacy advertising at older people. And indeed older people may be more concerned about making a Will than younger people. But if your charity has younger sup- porters, then persuading them to leave money to you is only a first step. You have to keep their support during their lifetime; you have to persuade them to give you more (to allow for in- flation) when they make a new Will; and you may have to wait very many years before you see a return for all this effort.

So whether you are encouraging older people or your younger supporters to leave money to you, legacy income is essentially long-term income. It is not something you think about in a cash crisis. But it can be an important part of your long-term fund- raising strategy. Anything you do now will help you secure your future.

### (b) Legacy income is received randomly

The only thing certain in life is death. But although death is certain, its timing is random. So your legacy income will depend on when the people who intend to leave you money actually die. For the larger charities the statistical probabilities will tend to even themselves out, and they will be able to predict fairly accurately the amount of legacy income that they will receive in any year. In fact of the top 25 charities (each with legacy income in excess of £1m per annum) virtually all have shown a year on year increase over the last five years and have seen their legacy income grow at near the average rate.

But for the smaller charities there can be significant fluctu- ations in what they receive from year to year. And if this is not anticipated it can cause problems, as the charity's own spending needs may require an even flow of money into its coffers.

There are two steps a charity can take to even out the fluctu- ations:

1. **Create an endowment fund.** If legacies are received as capital, and the income from the legacies is applied to the purposes of the charity, then however the legacies are received, the income from the endowment fund will rise from year to year. In fact legacies are an extremely good way of funding a capital endowment, as many lifetime donors prefer their money to be spent on the charity's present work, rather than being hoarded for the future.

And people leaving money in their Wills may like to see the benefit continue in perpetuity.

2. **Create a legacy equalisation account.** This is an accounting device where legacy income is not taken into the charity's income and expenditure account all at once, but a reserve is created with the sole purpose of evening out fluctuations from year to year. There are many ways of doing this.

In the example below we show one method of legacy equalisation. The legacy income received in any one year is divided into three parts; one third is taken into the accounts in the first year; one third in the second and one third in the third year. The example shows the effect of making such an equalisation, and the very random receipts have been largely evened out.

|      | Legacy income actually received | Equalised legacy income* |
|------|------|------|
| 1983 | 200,000 | 210,000 |
| 1982 | 230,000 | 160,000 |
| 1981 | 200,000 | 108,000 |
| 1980 | 50,000 | 75,000 |
| 1979 | 75,000 | 108,000 |
| 1978 | 100,000 | 100,000 |
| 1977 | 150,000 | 90,000 |
| 1976 | 50,000 | (* three year |
| 1975 | 70,000 | moving average) |

In fact legacy income is much more stable than you might tend to think. An analysis of the legacy income over a five-year period for 25 charities who received between £100,000 and £350,000 legacy income in 1981–82 shows:

14 charities had shown a 25% drop in income or more from one year to the next in at least one year over the five year period, but 11 had not.

Only 3 had not been on a rising trend.

In all cases the fluctuations would have been largely ironed out by some sort of equalisation procedure.

# LEGACY INCOME: SOME FACTS AND FIGURES

There is a further protection that a charity can have, and that is to avoid being overdependent on legacy income. Some of the larger charities do have a very substantial proportion of their total income received in the form of legacies:

| | |
|---|---|
| RSPCA | 71% |
| Imperial Cancer Research Fund | 59% |
| People's Dispensary for Sick Animals | 55% |
| Cancer Research Campaign | 54% |
| Dogs Home Battersea | 42% |

*The figures here relate to the proportion of total income including unearned income and earned income as well as grants and donations (voluntary income).*

Most charities will not obtain such a high proportion of their income in the form of legacy income. Normally legacies are just another source of income the charity receives, and this income helps contribute towards the charity's financial needs. Many smaller charities would be happy if they could get 10 per cent of their income from this source. And if they were to achieve 10 per cent, then if in any year the legacy income dropped by half, this would only result in a 5 per cent drop in the charity's overall income – which should not cause any real problems.

Although there are drawbacks to legacies as a source of income, there is also an overwhelming advantage. A substantial amount is given each year in the form of legacies, and we hope to show how to be successful in getting some of it in the chapters that follow. What is more, if charities were more active in soliciting legacy income from their supporters, the total of legacy income might rise very substantially from its present level of £260 million annually.

# PART II

# INCREASING YOUR LEGACY INCOME

# How to increase your legacy income

by Anthony Clay, Director (Sales and Funding), RSPB

Although the Royal Society for the Protection of Birds (RSPB) is one of the top 30 charities, it does not appear anywhere near the top of the league table for legacy income as yet. But we are putting this right.

The RSPB has shown quite remarkable growth in its legacy income in the last few years. Although with legacy income it is difficult to put anything to the test or to prove anything conclusively, I would like to draw out some lessons and some ideas from our attempts to raise the level of our legacy income, which I hope will be helpful to other charities trying to do the same.

I realise that the RSPB is a particular sort of charity with its own specific appeal. There may be big differences between the details of what we do and what others should do. But I do believe that the general principles remain the same.

The RSPB was formed in 1889. It was started by a group of people who were concerned about the importation of bird feathers for millinery purposes. It grew relatively slowly until the early 1950s, but dramatic growth occurred from the mid-1960s onwards. In 1963 we had 18,000 members. By 1982 we had over 350,000 members. We attribute this very substantial growth to a number of factors:

1. A great increase in public consciousness of the importance of wildlife conservation and the natural environment. Television has helped our cause enormously, as has the growth of colour printing. Perhaps above all the birdwatcher has

31

now become respectable – a David Attenborough or a Peter Scott, rather than some weird person disguised as a bush appearing from behind a bush.

2. The way we have approached the business of getting new members. Within the guidelines of our charter to develop public interest in birds, we have set about marketing ourselves aggressively and effectively.

Up until 1972 we had been receiving legacies at a fairly steady pace, but at a level of only about £50,000 a year. In the mid-1960s we undertook our first, very basic, research to see if we could improve our legacy income by simply asking our own solicitors what to do. I suggest that this was the most misleading research we could have carried out. We were told that there was no point advertising in legal journals because, in our solicitor's experience, he had never advised anybody on who to leave their money to, and he did not even remember ever having been asked for such advice. He suggested that we spent what money we had on publicising our organisation generally and not on advertisements specifically aimed at getting legacies.

Unfortunately we took this guidance and did practically nothing until the early 1970s.

However, in 1972, we learned from another charity that ever since they had started advertising for bequests, their legacy income had started to rise quite markedly. On the strength of this we thought that we ought to start a simple advertising campaign in a few legal journals and to develop our legacy appeal in our house magazine *Birds*. In due course we noted that our legacy income did in fact begin to rise.

## 1. Research: finding out more

Apart from the coincidence of the increase in RSPB legacy advertising and the growth in legacy income we had no way of linking the two. So, being a somewhat research-minded organisation, we decided that we should first of all try to find out a little more about our 'market'. We wanted to find out who was leaving money to us at that time and how they perceived us, what solicitors thought about us and how they might help us, and what type of person it was who was interested in leaving us a legacy. We undertook a number of different surveys, the results of which are discussed in the following paragraphs.

We found out that the way people perceived us was very different from how we perceived ourselves. When we conducted an analysis into 850 residuary legacies that we had received we found that, although we saw ourselves as a 'wildlife conservation' organisation, in 40 per cent of the cases where we shared legacies with other charity beneficiaries, the other charities were animal welfare charities and less than 4 per cent of them were charities concerned with wildlife conservation. So the very group with which we felt we should have been most closely identified turned out to be one of the least likely for us to share a legacy with.

Following on from this, we wanted to build a picture of a typical legator to help us in framing our appeal, so we analysed the legacies we had received during the previous two years and a number of interesting conclusions emerged. We found that:

1. The majority of those leaving us money were not, and apparently had not been, members of the RSPB. This may have been because of the inadequacy of our records, or simply because we did not go back far enough. Because there could have been a great many reasons for this, we were wary of drawing any firm conclusions; but it did seem that our legators were likely to have more of a general sympathy for what we do (or for animal welfare) rather than any firm commitment or involvement.

2. Those who had left us pecuniary (fixed sum) legacies were benefiting us far less than those who had left us a share of the residue of their estate. The difference was considerable, and it was certainly plain that we should try to put more effort into persuading people to leave us residuary legacies.

3. Eighty-one per cent of those leaving us money were female. Women live longer and so, not surprisingly, they were less likely than men to have a surviving spouse to whom to pass on the whole of their estate.

4. Of the residuary Wills we had received, a great majority had been made within five years and a very large number within two years. So if we could reach those people who were making their last Will, then we should see the benefits quite quickly.

5. Those people leaving us the residue of their estate (or a

share of it) by and large had no dependant relatives. This was no surprise, since it is quite understandable that charities benefit most when there are no dependants with prior claims to an estate.

From these researches, we were able to paint a picture of a typical RSPB legator. This is what we wrote:

*'Our typical legator will be single with no dependants or close family. She will be female, over 60, and will probably be very fond of animals. It is likely that she is a somewhat lonely person. She is quite possibly not a member of the RSPB. She is more likely to leave us a cash sum than a share of, or the whole of, the residue of her estate. She will have written a Will within the last five years of her life. For the administration of her estate, particularly if it is a large one, a Bank will probably be favoured. She probably will not have read any of our advertisements in the legal journals (although it is not unknown for solicitors or their clerks to give a charity supplement or directory to clients while they are waiting to make a Will or to help them decide which charities to benefit). If she is leaving us a large sum of money she will not be particularly impressed by whether or not we capitalise her legacy or use it for general purposes. There is evidence for us to believe that she thinks herself to be worse off than she really is (so the beneficiary is likely to benefit far more from a share in the residue than from a pecuniary legacy).*

*'There is also an important but quite different group of legators who might be contemplating a legacy of perhaps over £30,000. This group is much harder to define, and clearly there are far fewer people in this category. It is likely that they will have a fairly sophisticated attitude towards the distribution of their estate (because of the amount of money involved). They might well favour a charity which guaranteed to put their legacy towards capital projects.'*

In 1977 at the same time that we looked at our legators, we also looked at those people who were advising clients when they were drawing up their Will. What help did solicitors give in the choice of charity that a legator might benefit and how might we (the RSPB) reach those solicitors?

We took a sample of 174 solicitors who had been involved in drawing up Wills where the RSPB had been a named beneficiary. We wrote to them enclosing a questionnaire. We obtained 26 responses, a response rate of 15 per cent, which we felt was excellent in the circumstances and indicative of the concern that solicitors may feel in providing their clients with good advice. We provided no inducement (such as a free calendar) for the solicitor to reply. At a later date, we did test whether providing an inducement might increase the response rate, and we found that it did not do so appreciably.

Of those that did respond, we found that two solicitors had an extremely high level of interest in the RSPB and its work. One was a member of the RSPB and involved in a local group; the other was not then a member, which was remarkable – but we swiftly recruited him! For several years both these solicitors had been actively advising people to leave money to the RSPB whenever their views or advice were sought. These two solicitors have been directly responsible for obtaining a huge amount of legacy income for us.

From the other 24 replies we gleaned the following:

1. Very few people leave any money at all to charities in their Will. So any individual solicitor is seldom involved in having to check up on the correct name and address of a particular charity during the whole of his practising life.

2. When the client's Will was fairly straightforward, it was often not a partner of the firm who would deal with the client. It would probably be left to one of the clerks to do the drafting. The conclusion is obvious: it is not worth directing all your efforts at persuading the partners of the merits of your charity if they seldom or never get involved in the drafting of Wills. Indeed some solicitors do no probate work at all; and you should bear this in mind when planning 'broadside' promotions to the legal profession as a whole.

3. We tried to discover what literature solicitors read so that we could plan our advertising accordingly. The results were almost totally inconclusive, which probably means that one should advertise in all the relevant journals if one can afford to. It was generally felt that the legator knew precisely which charity she wished to benefit. Most solicitors (in the sample) said that they had never even heard of the publication 'Will to Charity', and none said that they had ever used it. Yet by a process of coding our address we know that we have had two very substantial legacies which we can

attribute directly to the advertisements we have placed in *'Will to Charity'*. So we know that advertising in *'Will to Charity'*, and in the other journals and directories, works for us, whatever solicitors may say about whether they find them useful or not.

4. We wanted to know whether solicitors felt that legators might prefer to leave their money for a capital project (in our particular case for the purchase of bird reserves), or whether they would be equally impressed by a charity which was putting its legacy income to general purposes (that is its administration, although we would never use that term!). They felt that most legators would be quite happy if their money went towards the general work of the charity. It would only be very rarely, and probably only in the case of a substantial legacy, that earmarking a legacy for a capital project would become attractive.

## 2. Action to increase legacy income

We produced a leaflet for enquirers and potential legators. This was a well thought out and attractive publication. It was something that people might want to obtain and to read, and not just a flimsy give-away. It was aimed at a broader audience than only those who were seriously contemplating leaving us a legacy. It had two functions: to stimulate people to make a Will and to leave us a legacy in that Will; and also to enable us to gauge the success of our advertisements in the different media we were using and with the different styles of advertising we might run. I believe that this was the single most important thing we did.

We advertised in new journals and tested other media, such as mail shots, which would communicate with potential legators more directly. One extremely successful medium for us was the magazine for the retired, *'Choice'*. We ran an advertisement offering a free booklet which combined the idea of leaving us a legacy with providing the reader with some leisure activity relevant to her – in this case the identification of garden birds and wildlife. This was an extremely cost-effective approach which often led to a subsequent sale of goods by our trading company (garden bird equipment, etc.).

We also decided to mail the trust offices of the Big Four clearing

**A RSPB leaflet encouraging supporters to leave a legacy.**

banks as they seemed to be involved in drawing up Wills and we had not reached them before.

At the same time as deciding to put more money into our advertising, we wanted to try to improve the style of our approach as much as we could. By testing different advertisements we were able to measure the response rates for different styles of advertising. We tried the following approaches (which are ranked in order of popularity):

1. Make friends with the birds.

2. Cruelty to birds, and in particular the plight of oiled seabirds.

3. Stewardship of our environment for our children – we should try to leave a land as rich in wildlife as we found it.

4. Research – help us to learn more about the manifold threats to wildlife.

5. A capital appeal for land purchase.

6. The tax advantages of leaving a legacy to a charity.

'*Make friends with the birds*' came out as being much the best approach. This was an advertising approach designed specifically for the typical legator we had previously defined. We went directly for what would appeal to her. We used such expressions as '*Friendship with the birds*' and slogans like '*Make friends with the birds*' and '*Your friends the birds*'. We reckoned that she would probably have garden birds that she was feeding, and that she would be very fond of them. Perhaps she would be more fond of her birds than of any living person – tragic, but true, for many. We coupled this approach with an illustration. We wanted a picture of birds that were appealing, helpless, friendless. We tried baby ducklings, but far better was a lone owl which seemed at the same time to be almost human.

The RSPB has grown to be a substantial membership organisation. In 1982 we had over 350,000 members and this had to be, and is, a prime target for us. One of our local groups of members ran a highly successful programme of visits to their bird reserve for the elderly. This was aimed at providing friendship, not at fund-raising. In fact it resulted in that group receiving quite large sums of money in the form of legacies.

Because we had discovered that solicitors could be of enormous

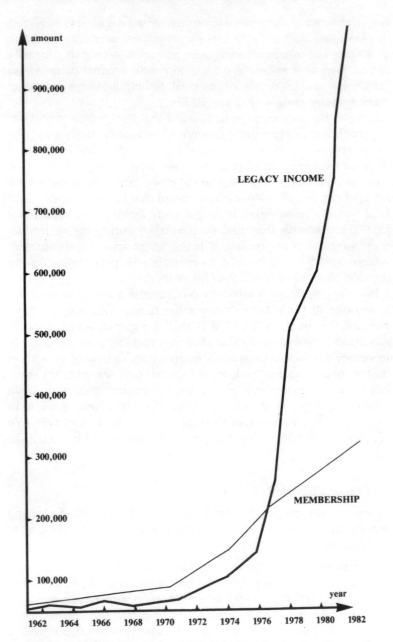

A table showing the growth of RSPB legacy income and membership over two decades.

help if they were committed to our cause, we decided to advertise in our house magazine *'Birds'* for solicitors, accountants, bank managers and others who might be prepared to help us generally in one way or another. We hope to create a panel of expertise which we can make use of, as well as helping these people to identify more closely with the RSPB.

Despite the fact that we had found that the 'capital donation' approach was not generally thought to be a particularly good one in our research with solicitors, and that it ranked low in the level of responses we had obtained in our advertising, we felt that some people might be persuaded to give a legacy to us only if we set up a capital fund. We also reckoned that these legacies might well be quite substantial. If people were leaving us a substantial part of the wealth they had accumulated during their lifetime, they might well appreciate it being spent on a capital project which would be of benefit to mankind in perpetuity. So we decided to set up a *'Land fund for birds'*.

It is very difficult to attribute our success directly to what we have done, as there are so many other factors which might have affected the situation. The RSPB itself has grown very substantially and we have seen the size of its membership increase sharply in recent years. We have tried to do a comparison of growth in legacy income and growth in membership to see whether there has been any expansion in our legacy income over and above what we might have expected simply from our growth in membership. I believe that the figures speak for themselves. We received £150,000 in legacies in 1976 and over £1,000,000 in 1982.

### 3. Lessons learned

From our experience I would like to draw out the following general points which I think are crucial for any charity seeking to increase the level of its legacy income:

1. **Know more about yourself** and who might be predisposed to give to you. Research for us paid off. We were able to define a target audience and get some indication as to how we might communicate with them. The research you do need not be expensive or necessarily time-consuming. If you can get some indication of how others perceive you, who might give to you and what they find attractive about

40

what you are doing, and if you can draw a thumbnail sketch of your potential legator, then you will be better placed to succeed in what you do.

2. **Tell your friends.** Tell all those who you are in contact with about what you are doing, and what your needs are, and how they might help you. We have had many people who were extremely happy to go out and do often quite hard physical labour at our bird reserves, but we had been failing to talk to them about financial matters. Talk to your supporters, your donors, your voluntary helpers, your members. These are the mainstay of your charity, the people who are committed to your cause and who might be predisposed to give to you.

3. **Advertise for legacies.** There may be some charities for whom this will be a complete waste of money. But for most, the proof is in the success of those who have tried it. Make sure you are in relevant publications, and that your advertising is as cost-effective as you can make it. Advertise in the legal journals. Advertise in any other place where you feel: (a) there is some relevance to your work, and (b) the audience consists of those people who might be interested in supporting you (with a legacy).

4. **Test your advertising.** This is a cardinal law of promotion. I do recommend to you the concept of the free booklet, so that you are not just getting people to fill in a form asking for further information. If you can supply them with something they might actually want or something which they would find really useful, then you will get a much higher response. This will not only serve you well for raising money and getting legacies, it will also enable you to assess the success of your advertising much more easily, and to continuously improve and refine your approach.

5. **Give your respondents someone to contact.** Perhaps provide a telephone service; some charities do this very successfully. Someone who might be interested in supporting you might want to talk to you about your work. In your advertising provide the name of somebody they can contact and, if possible, a telephone number for them to ring that person at. You can invent the name and use that as a method

of coding the advertisement and judging the success of your advertising – but the person should be real and your switchboard should know who to put the call through to.

6. **Respond to those people who contact you.** Respond very quickly and react very efficiently – not just to enquirers asking for your free booklet or more information, but also in the whole administration of your legacy business. There is nothing that will impress Executors more than the efficient and competent administration of legacies by you, and this can lead to them recommending their clients to leave their money to you.

7. **Persuade your respondents to support you.** Persuade them to leave you a residuary legacy in preference to a pecuniary legacy, but a pecuniary legacy is still better than nothing at all. If you have a younger audience, tell them about conditional bequests, where your charity is in the position of long stop should all else fail. Getting people to write your charity's name into their first Will, made perhaps when they first get married or have children, may mean that the name of your charity will continue to re-appear as a beneficiary in subsequent Wills. So do not be shy of asking for a legacy from those who have no intention of dying just yet!

8. **Do not be too shy** about asking for legacy income. Death is a taboo word and people find it distasteful to discuss how they are going to leave their money when they die. But I suggest that if people knew more about how much good charities can do (in relief of poverty, cure of disease, protection of the environment, etc.), then they would be more likely to leave a legacy to charity. In a sense a charity is providing a service by giving testators the opportunity to have their money survive them and to undertake good works beyond their grave. I suggest too that there is not just one single pool of legacy income available to charities, such that when all charities have discovered how to get hold of it they are all in competition with each other for a finite sum of money. I believe that what legators leave to charity is very small in relation to the value of their estates and what they might be persuaded to leave. Most people do not think of benefiting charities at the time they are making their Will;

those who do are, in fact, the exception. The task of charities is to persuade more people to give at least something and to persuade those who do give to give more. Remember REQUESTS EQUALS BEQUESTS. So do ask.

9. **Provide a specific cause for people to give to** if this is what they would like. If people wish to give you capital, then set up a capital fund or a capital appeal. Not everyone will want to make use of this, but some will. Nevertheless, discourage the earmarking of legacies to aspects of your work which are too specific. This can tie you down too much. If possible I would suggest to your legators that they include a form of wording which gives you the greatest freedom possible, 'perhaps including the phrase '*without creating a binding trust*'.

10. **Talk to lawyers.** I would encourage you to see if you have solicitors within your organisation – your membership, your Council, your trustees – who might be prepared to help you, and even to put in a good word for you with their clients. Do try to use any help they might give you, as it can make a staggering difference to the level of legacy income you receive. If you are a local charity, then contact all the solicitors in your area. This is not a hard job. If you are a national charity, you might consider writing to solicitors who have been involved in Wills where you were a beneficiary.

11. **Try to link together all the aspects of your work.** Your legacy work should not be conducted in isolation from your fund-raising, your promotion, your trading, your education. It should all be part of a whole. So often there is inadequate communication between the various departments of a charity. If you can, try to evolve a co-ordinated approach. Success in getting legacy income is part of building a successful organisation, and building a successful organisation will in turn help you to get more legacy income.

# Advertising for legacy income

by Philip Mellor, Westmore Advertising

About one third of all gifts to charity made by individuals are made at death; and despite growing calls on disposable capital, legacies remain the fastest growing sector of charitable revenue. It is not surprising therefore that many charities take full advantage of this extremely fruitful way of obtaining money for their work

Top of the league – and it will come as no surprise – is Imperial Cancer Research Fund with over £8 million, representing nearly 80% of its voluntary income, and the second largest individual sum is the £7 million obtained by the Cancer Research Campaign. But then cancer is the most emotive word in the charity world, and all cancer charities seem to do rewardingly well.

Due to that sentimental quirk about animals in the British character – especially amongst women – the RSPCA currently obtains as much as 95% of its voluntary income from legacies, some £5 million per annum. And amongst the lesser charities, though much smaller in actual amount, the Battersea Dogs Home obtains 94% of its voluntary income from the same source, with (as far as I can detect) the minimum of expenditure.

The Salvation Army has also achieved an enormous increase in its legacy income over the past few years, due no doubt to the immense respect in which it is held by a wide spectrum of the populace for the dedicated way it genuinely looks after the down and outs, and the heart-warming, almost ingenuous way, it raises its money. There is a parallel to a certain extent with the success the Cheshire Homes has achieved in attracting legacy income, in that Leonard Cheshire, its charismatic founder, has become such a loved and much admired person by the public at large.

But it isn't only the better known, highly emotive charities which have been so successful in tapping this immensely valuable source of revenue. There are a number of smaller and lesser known charities which do remarkably well in terms of the percentage of their voluntary incomes that they obtain in the form of legacies:

| | |
|---|---|
| Distressed Gentlefolk's Aid Association | 83% |
| Royal UK Benificent Association | 81% |
| Musicians Benevolent Fund | 77% |
| Methodist Homes for the Aged | 75% |
| Royal National Institute for the Deaf | 69% |
| Scottish Nat. Inst. for the War Blinded | 64% |
| Chest, Heart and Stroke Association | 61% |
| King George's Fund for Sailors | 61% |

No doubt there are many others who achieve way above the 30% average! And though I have no first hand facts and figures to go on, most of the above appear to achieve these remarkable results with the minimum of expenditure. None of them is a cancer charity and none is particularly well known. So smaller charities – and indeed local charities – may be able to get substantial legacy income at relatively small cost, if they set their minds to it.

By now, it must be obvious that legacies are an extremely important potential source of funds. But in no way will the money just miraculously appear. You actually have to do something to steer it your way.

### 1. Legacies are a long-term investment

To give an example of how making a modest investment can help you increase your legacy income, let me cite the case of the British Heart Foundation (BHF). In 1976 the BHF's legacy income amounted to around £500,000 annually, representing 30% of its voluntary income; and there is every reason to believe that it would have stayed at around this level (in real terms) had no action been taken.

But the BHF did decide to do something. The first thing they did was to appoint my advertising agency as their consultants. Right from the beginning, I strongly recommended that they should consider making a modest but positive attack on this particular market segment. They agreed, and each year we gradually strengthened the attack as the budget increased, with the result that by 1982, the BHF was getting £3.1 million annually in legacies, representing some 54% of its voluntary income.

I am well aware that there were certain external factors which probably contributed to this considerable rise. Certainly the high incidence of heart disease, and the fact that it causes more deaths than all other major causes of death put together, has become much more widely known; and in any case the BHF had always pursued a lively policy of prospecting for *'In Memoriam'* donations. Nevertheless, getting more legacy income was a direct consequence of their decision to **do something positive about it**.

When it comes to making the difficult decision whether or not to devote some of your much needed and hard won income to this particular type of fund raising, there are certain important considerations you should have in the forefront of your mind.

1. You need a high input of faith. If you undertake a membership drive you can quickly measure your success by the number of members you recruit. Legacy advertising is different. Like a good gardener, you never know when you will reap the fruits of the seeds you sow. It may take years – like most worthwhile fruits! All I can say is that in general those charities that have advertised have succeeded. And those that have not (with the few notable exceptions already mentioned above) have not.

2. Legacy income is not instant income. It is generally held that the average time between someone making their last Will and dying, is four years. So if you are advertising to persuade people to leave money to you, it could take up to seven years between the start of your campaign and a regular flow of income.

3. Not every charity is likely to be successful in attracting income. It very much depends on the nature of the work you do and how appealing it is. Small charities active in dealing with drug addiction, equal opportunities for women or community arts, for example, are not likely to appeal strongly to the aged affluent, who must be the prime (but not the only) target for legacy income. It is important

therefore that you look quite objectively at your cause and determine whether or not it is likely to succeed.

4.  Of course, if you create – or have already created – a strong public awareness of your cause through your public relations or paid-for press advertising activities, you will find it that much easier. And many of those charities that were well known in the past may still be well known by the older members of the public, who after all, are the ones that matter when it comes to legacies. The converse of course, is that if you are not well known, you may have to work twice as hard.

5.  Unlike prospecting for donations generally, it is not that costly to go after legacy income. And for any charity, even with only limited funds, I would certainly advise allocating a reasonable proportion of whatever fund raising budget is available towards this objective. It should be regarded, literally, as an investment in the future of the charity.

## 2. How to go about obtaining legacy income

Let us assume that you have come to the conclusion that you are the sort of charity that could attract at least some legacy income (and this will be the case for most charities that are doing anything worthwhile). What actually do you do then?

The first thing is to think about what you can do in order to attract this particular type of income. But remember, whatever you decide to do should be seen in the context of your organisation as a whole. Taking action to get legacy income will be more successful if you have a positive approach to the overall development of your organisation and its public image.

You have to decide how to set about trying to influence those who are drawing up their Wills and those who might be persuaded to add a Codicil to an existing Will. I think that there are three main areas where you should direct your efforts:

1.  Continually strive to keep your name and the importance of your cause in front of those who advise (and may even have some influence) on the drawing up of Wills – that is solicitors certainly, bankers to a certain degree, and accountants very occasionally.

2.  By a drip-drip-drip process, instil the thought of giving

money to your charity into the minds of those who are about to die – primarily the well-souled and well-heeled ageing.

3. Ensure that *explicit* literature is sent to all your donors, your members and your activists, and that such literature is distributed at all functions and events you organise.

## 3. Influencing the professionals

The legal profession, and specifically solicitors, are your most important target. You can reach them through the specialist trade magazines. There are several of these. So which do they read? It is always a problem when you have to decide to use one particular magazine and not another, as each solicitor will have his own individual preferences. But short of canvassing the whole profession, the only safe way (if you have the money to do this), is to stretch your budget across the range of publications. The cost will not be that great.

Each of the main law publications has created a specialist vehicle for charity advertising. These are:

**New Law Journal Annual Charities Review** *(April)*
**New Law Journal Christmas Appeals Supplement** *(November)*
**Solicitors Journal Charity Appeals Supplement** *(November)*
**Law Society's Gazette Charity Review Supplement** *(November)*

In addition, there are three other specialist publications:

**Will to Charity** – **The Charities Story Book** *(June)*
**Will to Charity** – **Regional Directory** *(November)*
**Family Welfare Association's Charities Digest** *(March)*

The basic details are as follows:

(a) *Distribution:* the *New Law Journal, Solicitors Journal* and *Law Society's Gazette,* are sold by subscription only. Subscribers receive the charity supplements automatically. The *Law Society's Gazette* is sent to every member of the Law Society which includes all qualified solicitors and achieves by far the largest circulation – though it is debatable how appropriate this extended readership is and whether it justifies the considerably higher cost.

Both the issues of *Will to Charity* are sent free to solicitors' offices, banks, public reference libraries and chartered accountants. And unlike the law journals which circulate only in England and Wales, *Will to Charity* is distributed in Scotland and Northern Ireland as well. *Charities Digest* – useful though it is – has the drawback that it has to be bought, so there is no assurance that it reaches the whole target market.

(b) *Format: Will to Charity* and the *Charities Digest* are produced in book form. This smaller format is easier to handle and sits happily on a bookshelf. The chances of these publications being kept and used is therefore that much greater. All the others are magazine size.

(c) *Publication date:* As you will have noticed, the majority of the legal special supplements are published in the late Autumn, and it could be argued that being so near Christmas and associated with Christmas appeals, they might not be quite so effective as they might be if published at some other time. The *New Law Journal Annual Charity Review* for instance, comes out in the Spring and *Will to Charity Story Book* in June.

Full details of these publications are given in the next section. They are your basic media, and you should seriously consider advertising in all of them if you are determined to prospect for legacies. If you had to limit your choice, I would incline towards the *New Law Journal Annual Charity Review* published in the Spring, and the *Will to Charity Story Book* published in June.

If you have the money, you should also consider putting a small space advertisement into all or some of the legal journals on a regular basis. For just as you never know when a legacy will drop into your lap, so you cannot know the moment when a solicitor or banker may be consulted about the drawing up of a Will, or the making of a Codicil.

If you are interested in reaching Scotland, the law journals published in England do not get there. There is a separate legal system for Scotland, and separate magazines to cater for it:

**Scottish Law Gazette**
**Scots Law Times**
**Journal of the Law Society of Scotland**

Of these only the *Scots Law Times* produces a special charity supplement. If you do advertise in a Scottish law publication, do give an address in Scotland. It will increase the response you get quite remarkably. If your charity does not have a branch or an office in Scotland, then use a post-box or an accommodation address. A Scottish publisher or local law firm will probably be willing to provide this service for you.

Solicitors are not the only professional people to assist in the drawing up of Wills. The 'Big 4' clearing banks are becoming increasingly involved. They may provide a less personal service than the local solicitor, and may be that much more difficult to influence. But if you decide that the banks are an important target audience for you, then the following two publications are worth considering:

**The Banker**

**Bankers Magazine**

Some people suggest that the accountancy profession might possibly be a suitable target for legacy advertising. There is no evidence that accountants do assist in the drawing up of Wills, and my experience is that advertising to accountants is money wasted. I would not recommend it.

In general put your money where it is going to work. There are always people presenting you with opportunities to part with your hard-won cash – publishers of annuals, yearbooks, diaries and all kinds of miscellaneous nefarious enterprises. None of them is likely to work as well as the specialist media for legacy advertising that I have mentioned; and if you concentrate on those, you will not be the loser. There are of course, exceptions to every rule, and you must use your own judgement. The *Daily Mail Yearbook* for instance, has worked well for me in the past for general donations advertising.

### 4. Making the most of your investment

If you do decide to spend money on advertising, there are a few important points you should bear in mind:

1. **Getting noticed:** Around 400 charities, for example, advertise each year in the *Law Society's Gazette Charity Review Supplement*; so you should obviously try to do everything you can to make sure that your advertisement stands

out in the crowd. It may well be worth your while to spend a little extra money in order to achieve a premium space. These are some of the positions I would recommend:

Back cover (but inside back cover is too much at the back of the book).

Inside front cover.

Facing contents page or index.

Facing section index (if the publication is sectionalised).

Near the front of the book.

Near the front of the section (if the publication is sectionalised)

2. **Getting the message right:** All too often a charity will send in an advertisement that has been used for a completely different purpose, just because it is available. It may be quite wrong for legacy prospecting and work far less well than it could; it may even be designed for a different-sized space – and I have seen instances of advertisements placed sideways on the page. Try to ensure that the advertisement you are paying for is designed for the purpose it is serving. I will elaborate more on this later.

3. **Monitoring the response:** You will only be able to decide if an advertisement is working well for you if you have some means of identifying those responses that have stemmed from that particular advertisement. As with all charity advertising, it is useful to have this information as a means of comparing different media, and to draw inferences which might help you plan your advertising better in the future. So try to insert some detail in the advertisement which will appear in the reply. In the case of legacies, this probably means information that is actually written into the Will. If the detail is changed in each advertisement then you have a workable coding system. For legacies it is best to code the address. This would then appear in the Will in the form: 'I give £..... to ..... (name of charity and registration number) of ..... (address of charity)'. The address could be coded as Room WTC/1, or Room 22, or 117/c Golden Avenue – or whatever.

## 5. Other ways of approaching solicitors

Advertising in the legal journals is not the only way to reach solicitors. It works best for the larger charity working on a national basis and with a fairly wide appeal. For a local charity which is of purely local interest, there are a number of other possibilities which might be considered, either instead of, or in addition to, paid-for advertisements.

1. **Direct mailing:** Sending the information direct to your target solicitors, with a letter which is interesting and intriguing enough from the first paragraph, to prevent it being thrown straight into the waste paper basket.

2. **Direct approach:** At a local level (and also nationally), you can try to contact solicitors in person to state your case. The Spastics Society have a programme of writing to solicitors requesting an interview and over 40% of the people written to have responded positively, often with a partner of the firm giving an appointment of up to an hour. The presentation is well prepared and the charity is able to show what it is doing, the importance of its work and what sort of help it needs. The investment needed for this approach (except at a local level, when it is much more easy to organise) is quite substantial; but it is a highly effective method of communicating.

3. **Through your supporters:** Amongst your membership and supporters there will be a fair sprinkling of solicitors. These will be already aware of what you are doing, and to some degree committed to your cause. You can reach them quite easily and ask them to use their influence in advising their clients to your advantage, should they be asked for advice.

4. **Using gimmicks:** Some charities have tried sending calendars, blotters, jotters, diaries, pens and other giveaways to solicitors to try and curry their favour. It is doubtful how effective such a relatively expensive ploy might be, but if you feel it might work for you, then it is worth considering.

Perhaps the most important factor of all, is the image you present to solicitors in your dealings with them. If you are getting any legacy income at all, you will be in correspondence with executors

52

or trustees fairly regularly. If you are courteous, efficient and professional in your dealings, you will present an indelible image of being a charity which is not only doing good, but doing good effectively. And if a solicitor sees you are competent, it will greatly enhance the likelihood that he will advise in your favour again and again.

## 6. Reaching the aged affluent

It is much more difficult and much more expensive to reach out and influence the general public than it is to tackle a small and well-defined section of the population such as solicitors.

If you do allocate money to advertising, it is understandable that you will probably wish to devote most of your effort to attracting general donations and building up a large and immensely valuable mailing list, which you can then use in a whole variety of ways to bring in still more income.

But since the whole purpose of any publicity campaign is to heighten the general awareness of your charity and the importance of your cause, it will naturally also influence people's inclination to leave you something in their Will.

If you can't afford a major advertising campaign then consider placing classified advertisements regularly in selected national newspapers as often as your finances will allow. One of the large cancer charities does this all the time. Repetition is important because by the drip-drip-drip process you instil yourself on to the public's consciousness. Whether you should run the same advertisement each week or whether you should vary the theme is open to debate. Some people feel that a repetition of exactly the same wording each week will eventually force the message through; others hold that people will stop looking at the advertisement because they feel they have already read it. Whichever point of view you adopt – consistency, or change, or a mixture of the two – be sure that what you say is concise, well-written, clearly stated and compelling.

Charity advertising is a subject in itself, but I propose to offer a few basic tips here. For further information and ideas see the handbook on 'Charity Advertising' also published by the Directory of Social Change.

**The popular press:** Forget it. Circulation may be high, but then, so is the self-indulgence factor, resulting inevitably in a low response. Readers of the 'heavy' press on the other hand not only appear to 'care' rather more, but usually have more to dispose of anyway.

**Daily Telegraph:** It used to be said that 80% of all charitable donations came from women over sixty who read the Daily Telegraph. It may once have been true, but inflation has changed this. Although the *Daily Telegraph* is likely to work well, it is not 'the one and only' medium that it used to be.

**Sunday Telegraph:** In my experience, this is a good medium, and it does after all reach virtually the same readership as the *Daily Telegraph* in a less crowded way and on a 'leisure' day.

**The Times:** For legacies I would still keep this in the schedule occasionally, although I would not use it for general fundraising.

**Financial Times:** No. I would not consider it either for legacy or for general advertising, even though they often give two insertions for the price of one.

**Observer:** The *Observer* is very much a 'caring' paper and I would tend to have this in the schedule.

**Guardian:** Similar to the *Observer*, it is good on donations and many charities use it. But less good on legacies, probably because of its younger readership. The young, active and caring are probably less prepared to think that far ahead, and the money would take too long to come in anyway.

**Daily Mail:** Good for display advertising but rather crowded for classifieds and I would put a question mark over it.

**Sunday Times:** I would put a big question mark over this too. Although it reaches the right market, it is expensive and the classified sections are so huge your advertisement may tend to get lost.

**Magazines:** On the whole forget these altogether. Some charities claim success with *The Lady*. I find that the *Methodist Recorder* always seems to work for donations for any charity, but the return is modest. Most religious papers tend to return very little, other than for highly emotive causes and their own denominations – which is understandable.

**Radio and TV appeals:** At the moment charities are not permitted to pay to advertise for funds on the broadcast media

A range of small ads used by charities for advertising for legacy income.

other than through the appeal slots, which are free. These provide an immediate and very high return, and they can and do have an influence on public attitudes and how people dispose of their money for charitable purposes. These are available on application; but because of the limited air time available, demand far outstrips allocation.

**Companies:** It is possible to mail the Chairmen or Managing Directors of the large companies. Their addresses are in the *Times Top 1000* list – if you can afford to buy it. But it is difficult to influence these people. Most of them anyway, are in touch with charities through the donations programmes of their companies. So if they haven't already made up their minds how they are going to dispose of their money, they are probably not going to leave anything to charity at all. If you do wish to reach this audience, a direct personal approach will work immeasurably better than a mailing or advertisements in such magazines as *The Director* or *Management Today*.

## 7. Rationalising the cost

It is easy enough to generalise about particular media and opportunities. It is far harder to use this information to build a successful promotional campaign and then monitor each advertisement to evaluate how well it has performed, both in terms of the advertisement itself and the medium in which it appeared.

And never judge your investment purely by the ratio of cost to direct return that you achieve. You need to look at your response in a much more enlightened way, as part of a strategy of building your organisation. After all, it is the Income and Expenditure account at the end of the year that is important in assessing the value of your investment, not how well or badly a particular advertisement appeared to do.

The 'act of faith' I mentioned at the beginning is just as relevant to expenditure on general advertising as it is to taking the decision to spend on advertising for legacies. The only difference is that with legacies, you have to wait several years to know how successful your advertising has been! This makes meaningful analysis that much harder, and means that a lot of guesswork is involved.

Unlike prospecting for public support generally, prospecting for legacies specifically need not be a vastly expensive business.

If you are really serious about it, you should aim to allocate around 10% of your advertising budget to this particular sector. If your funds are limited then you should consider allocating whatever you can afford, depending on the sort of charity you are and your target audience. But if you consider that the average legacy income for those that get it is over 30% of their total income, it gives an indication of the sort of allocation you should be thinking about. The minimum you would need to spend in my opinion, would be around £650.

### 8. Persuading your supporters

Your supporters, past and present, represent a prime target for getting legacies. They have already demonstrated their support for your charity and should not be too difficult to persuade to remember you in their Will. Because you are in touch with them, they are easy to reach. Because they support what you are doing, they are more likely to give to you and to give to you substantially. The only problem is that some of them may be young, not yet ready to die – even for your cause! But it is certainly worth making an effort, even if the pay-back period is slightly longer.

In this connection I would like to suggest that you do a few simple things; and it is surprising how many charities fail to do them:

1.  In all your literature hammer home the point that you need money, that if people give you money it will be well spent, and that a legacy is a particularly effective way of supporting the charity. Tell your supporters about ways of giving to you in everything you produce and send out, even in your Annual Report. If you can't afford space to display the appropriate forms, make a brief reference and say that you will provide further information on request.

2.  Produce a special leaflet entitled 'Ways of giving . . !. This can include information on:

    Membership

    Donations via Deed of Covenant

    Large gifts (with tax relief details)

    Legacies, including a guide to the wording of bequests

Will making
simply
explained

OXFAM

What should I do
when someone dies?

A practical guide

One day, sooner or later, you are probably
going to have to comfort and look after a
friend or a relative who has lost someone
close. You yourself perhaps are facing just
such a loss now. Grief and emotion may mean
you feel bewildered and unable to cope.
The laws and regulations that say what has
to be done when someone dies are many and
complex. This little guide only aims to give
you general guidance and is not comprehensive, but we hope it will at least point you in
the right direction if more expert advice or
help are needed. It is correct as at June
1982.

Your will
and how it could help
some of the poorest
people on earth.

A range of leaflets and booklets produced by Oxfam which aim to
encourage people to leave money for Oxfam and provide general
information on Will-making and on what to do when someone
dies. These can be simply printed in one or two colours and need
not be expensive to produce.

Leaflets and booklets produced by several leading charities on ways of giving. This information which can also include sample wording for legacies and covenant forms can also be reproduced as part of a charity's annual report. A good way to compile your own brochure is to use what other charities produce as a starting point.

59

This leaflet need not be expensive to produce. It can be enclosed with any acknowledgement of a donation. It can be given out at functions or left lying around your office for visitors to pick up. This sort of promotion is infinitely more cost-effective than any paid-for advertising. Indeed if you are large enough (or ambitious enough) you may even consider producing a booklet on 'Making a Will . . .'.

## 9. Creating the advertisement

I would like to conclude by looking a little at what you should be saying in your advertisement. 'Form follows function' was a catchword in twentieth century architecture and it is equally applicable to advertising. The function of an advertisement is to persuade someone to do something. Who they are and what you want them to do will vary. So how do you compose a good advertisement? I would offer the following basic advice:

**Keep it simple.**

**Keep to the point.** Don't waste words.

**Don't be clever clever.** But be creative. And try to think of ways in which your advertisement can stand out in the crowd and be noticed.

**State the facts.** People want to know what the charity is, what it does, why the work is important. Lawyers also need to know the full name and address of the charity and the charity registration number, so they can be included in the Wills they are drawing up.

**Tell people what you want them to do.** You want the reader to respond; make it easy for them to do so.

**Include a coding,** if you can, so that you can analyse the success of a particular advertisement and of the medium in which it appears.

Here are two legacy appeal advertisements I wrote for the British Heart Foundation which I feel illustrate these points extremely well. The first is a classified advertisement:

*'I give and bequeath. . . .' Since more people die from heart disease than from all other illnesses put together, a legacy or bequest towards heart research could save the lives of so many others in the future.*
*British Heart Foundation, 57 Gloucester Place, London W1H 4DH*

The other, which is reproduced on the following pages together with half a dozen others which I regard as equally good, was conceived specifically for the specialist media for legacy advertising:

### Life. After death

*Legacies are a way of giving life after death because they help to finance research.*

*And we have proved over the last eighteen years that research does save lives.*

*This is particularly important in the case of heart disease, which still kills off as many as one in two of us – over twice as many as die from cancer.*

*The only way in which to bring about a significant reduction in deaths is to finance even more research.*

*That's why we are asking for your support, because legacies are without doubt the most rewarding way of contributing to our cause. Both for those who give and we who receive.*

*If you would like more information please ring. . . .*

Life – after death. That is what bequeathing is basically about. The passing on – after you have passed on – of hope and help to those less fortunate than yourself; benefiting some society or charity which champions some interest or belief you hold; remembering those who have a disability or need similar to one you had to face; as compensation for some of the things you have failed to achieve in your own lifetime; in memory of some close friend or spouse who died of a particular disease or affliction; in gratitude for the good life you have enjoyed; or in perpetuating your own memory beyond the grave. These are some of the ways in which making a legacy can be more than just giving money away. If people can achieve a sense of fulfilment through their legacy giving, we can help them to do this. If we understand why people want to give, we can all the better encourage them to give.

And surely, this is what we're all about – each in his own way. Helping to fill the gap that government bodies can't and won't fill, so that those in need of care and support and protection can receive it. And we know that raising money to bridge that gap is no easy matter nowadays and needs all the skill and dedication that can be brought to bear. I hope you will find the advice I have given constructive and that it will help you achieve the long-term financial security you need if you are to further the aims and ambitions of the cause you serve.

On the following pages are a number of advertisements that charities use. The ones selected were all used in publications aimed at the legal profession and were produced specifically to encourage people to leave legacies and to encourage solicitors to advise their clients on the merits of the particular charity. This range shows the variety of styles and the sort of information that can be included when advertising for legacies.

# After death.

Legacies are a way of giving life after death, because they help to finance research.

And, as we've proved over the last 18 years, research **does** save lives.

This is particularly important in the case of heart disease which still kills off one in every two of us – over twice as many as die from cancer.

The only way to bring about a significant reduction in deaths, is to finance even more research.

That's why we are asking for your support, because legacies are without doubt the most rewarding way of contributing to our cause – both for those who give and we who receive.

If you would like literature, please ring **01-935 0185**

## HEART RESEARCH
### does save lives

**British Heart Foundation,**
57 Gloucester Place, London W1H 4DH.

SUDBURY HALL, DERBYSHIRE.

# Some clients' legacies are forgotten in months.... but some will leave their mark for centuries

If your client appreciates this country's heritage – then over 150 houses, 88 gardens, 450,000 acres of coastline and countryside, much of the best from our past, can benefit from your help.

The Trust has powers from Parliament to protect for all time. A legacy to help the Trust fulfil its task is surely one of the most satisfying dispositions you can draft for your clients.

Recent Finance Acts have provided that all gifts and legacies to the Trust of whatever size are exempt from Capital Gains Tax, Capital Transfer Tax and aggregation. In this way, a legacy to the National Trust is unusually effective in serving your client's good intention precisely, without Government intervention through taxation. Every penny left to us goes direct to help the work of the National Trust.

If you would like to know more about the National Trust (registered charity no. 205846), please contact:– The Solicitor, The National Trust for Places of Historic Interest or Natural Beauty, 42 Queen Anne's Gate, London SW1H 9AS.
Tel: (01) 222 9251

## The National Trust

Help us to preserve the past for the future

# Help for all the nation's blind

When the RNIB is named as a legatee or receives an annual Deed of Covenant, the benefit goes to all Britain's 130,000 blind people. Our services reach them in every part of the United Kingdom; our research activities cover all aspects of blindness and its prevention.

Your advice and guidance to clients in the drawing up of bequests in our favour– pecuniary or residuary– is of the utmost importance to our work to educate, rehabilitate and train Britain's blind people, whoever and wherever they are.

# ROYAL NATIONAL INSTITUTE FOR THE BLIND

ROOM 54 GREAT PORTLAND STREET, LONDON W1N 6AA

Under the Finance Act 1975, bequests to charities up to a total of £250,000 are exempt from Capital Transfer Tax, Registered in accordance with the National Assistance Act 1948, and under the Charities Act 1960 (Reg. No. 226227).

# DO YOU HAVE THE WILL TO FIGHT CANCER?

The Imperial Cancer Research Fund is one of the world's leading cancer research centres.

Day in, day out, leading specialists in cancer research continue their intensive investigations into all aspects of cancer–causes, prevention, treatment and–ultimately–cure.

The continuation of this urgent work is solely dependent on public support–75% of which is derived from legacies.

So when testators ask your advice, remember the Imperial Cancer Research Fund. And help fight cancer with a will.

**Form of Bequest**

I hereby bequeath the sum of............pounds free of duty to the Imperial Cancer Research Fund, Lincoln's Inn Fields, London WC2A 3PX for the purpose of scientific research, and I direct that the receipt of the Honorary Treasurer or Secretary shall be a good discharge for such legacy.

Please write for further information to:
The Secretary, I.C.R.F., PO Box 123,
Room No. 503/4
Lincoln's Inn Fields,
London WC2A 3PX

## IMPERIAL CANCER RESEARCH FUND

**Fight cancer with a will**

Patron: H.M. THE QUEEN
President:
The Honourable Angus Ogilvy

66

THE WILL TO LIVE

*Last Will and Testament of ———, being of sound mind + body. I give to the SAVE THE CHILDREN Fund, at 157 Clapham Rd. LONDON SW9.0PT the sum of £———, and I direct that the receipt of the Treasurer for the time being or other duly authorised Officer will be sufficient discharge to my Executor.*

*Signed:*
*Date:*

*Witnesses:*

Your legacy to Save the Children could give a child in this country or the third world their only chance. If you would like to know more about our work for children at home and overseas write to Peter Lindsey at the address below.

# Save the Children
**The Save the Children Fund, 157 Clapham Road, London SW9 0PT.**

# Barnardo's can count on limitless goodwill. We also need money.

We have a legacy of more than 9,000 children bequeathed to us by many different people. Although we are determined to do everything we can to help our children, there is one single numbing difficulty. Cost. This year it will cost nearly £23 million to run our homes, schools, day care centres and family services.

A major part of our funds comes from legacies from kind people who feel interest in our work. And many of them first consider Barnardo's because of a suggestion made by someone like you.

If you have helped us in the past, please accept our heartfelt thanks. If you can help us in the future it could mean that children who would otherwise have no hope will grow up to be happy and well-adjusted adults.

If you would like to have more details about our work, please contact us.

**Barnardo's**

Barnardo's, Tanners Lane, Barkingside, Ilford, Essex IG6 1QG.
Telephone: 01-550 8822

69

*The NCH is a national charity based in London. This advertisement appeared in a Scottish publication; note that it contains a Scottish address.*

# Advertising in legal publications

In this section we give the basic details of all the main law publications that charities can use to advertise to the legal profession. In most cases the publishers produce special advertising supplements which contain charity advertising. However, charities can (and some do) advertise in the regular issues of these magazines as well.

The details given include:

1. **Name** of the publication.

2. **Address and telephone number** for enquiries about advertisements.

3. **Format**, including the size of the publication, method of binding and type area on page.

4. **Readership**: the audited readership figure is given, and where these are not produced, an estimate has been obtained from the publisher. The figures are the latest available, in most cases for 1982.

5. **Cost**: the cost is given for display advertising of different sizes. Except for the Charities Digest all the advertising is zero-rated for Value Added Tax. The rates given apply for 1983. Details of rates for special positions (e.g.: back cover, facing inside front cover, etc.) and any discounts that are available can be obtained from the address given.

6. **Further information** about the publication.

*(Editor's note: The information given in this section is impartially given, and no payment has been received from any of the publishers of the directories and supplements listed.)*

pages of 'editorial' matter can be purchased for £240. All advertisers in the 'Charities Story Book' are also given a free listing in the November edition of 'Will to Charity' (see below).

## WILL TO CHARITY: THE CHARITIES STORY BOOK
(June issue)

10 Beauchamp Place,
London SW3 1NQ
*Telephone: 01–589 6716
and 01–584 3039*

**Publication date:** June.

**Format:** 210mm × 148mm (A5); paperback (perfect bound). Type area: 182mm × 118mm.

**Readership:** free distribution of 10,000 print run to: Solicitors in England, Scotland, Wales and Northern Ireland; Trustee offices of banks in the UK; Public libraries; Chartered accountants in the UK; and Libraries of British Embassies and Representatives throughout the world.

**Cost:** Full-page advertisement plus one full page of 'editorial' matter £485; ½-page advertisement plus ½-page of 'editorial' matter £280.

The 'editorial' matter is supplied by the charity. The charity can, if it wishes, combine its advertisement and the editorial matter into what is effectively one large advertisement. Additional

## WILL TO CHARITY: CHARITIES BY COUNTIES AND REGIONS (November issue)

10 Beauchamp Place,
London SW3 1NQ
*Telephone: 01–589 6716
and 01–584 3039*

**Publication date:** November.

**Format and Readership:** as for 'Will to Charity: the Charities Story Book'.

**Cost:** Listing of charity giving name, address, telephone number, charity registration number plus 30 words of copy £42.

**Cost of display advertising:**
½-column including 2 free listings £142; 1/3-column including 1 free listing £102; (other rates on request).

Basic details of charities are listed by geographical area and county. Only charities who pay are listed in this publication.

# ADVERTISING IN LEGAL PUBLICATIONS

## CHARITIES DIGEST

Family Welfare Association,
501–505 Kingsland Road,
London E8 4AU
*Telephone: 01–254 6251*

**Publication date:** end-November (1984 edition published in November 1983, etc.).

**Format:** 210mm × 129mm (slightly narrower than A5); paperback (perfect bound). Type area: 173mm × 105mm.

**Readership:** Purchase price is £6.25. Subscribers include reference libraries, trustee departments of banks, legal advisers and other organisations. The Charities Digest is circulation to every Citizens Advice Bureau in the country and to some local authority Social Services Departments. It is also available through bookshops. The print run is 6,000, and the publishers expect to distribute the whole of this. Unlike the other media for legacy advertising, this publication is sold rather than given away free or distributed as a supplement to readers of a magazine.

**Cost:** Full-page £130; ½-page £70.
Note: Because the *Charities Digest* is only published annually, it is not covered by the zero-rating for advertising in newspapers and in periodicals and VAT is payable on the advertising charges. The prices given here exclude VAT.

The *Charities Digest* contains details of the names, addresses, telephone numbers and up to 250 words outlining the work of the charity. Information is supplied by the charities themselves. Entries in the Digest are not dependent on whether the charity takes advertising space.

To be listed in this publication, a charity has to be approved by a Committee set up by the publisher. The charities that are listed are mainly national and London-based organisations. Any charity not listed which feels that it should be listed should apply to the Family Welfare Association. The basic entry is free and additional information is printed at a charge of £3 (plus VAT) per column-inch, with a minimum charge of £6.

A charity wishing to take a display advertisement in this publication is required to submit an application for listing. And only if it is approved by the Committee will it be allowed to advertise.

## THE LAW SOCIETY'S GAZETTE: CHARITY AND APPEALS DIRECTORY

The Law Society, 113 Chancery Lane, London WC2A 1PL
*Telephone: 01-242 1222*

**Publication date:** end-November.

**Format:** 297mm × 210mm (A4); perfect bound (magazine with spine). Type area: 267mm × 184mm.

**Readership:** Free to subscribers to the Law Society's Gazette to more than 40,000 solicitors in England and Wales.

**Cost:** Full-page £700; $\frac{1}{2}$-page £360; $\frac{1}{4}$-page £200; $\frac{1}{8}$-page £120; $\frac{1}{16}$-page £65.

Every advertiser is entitled to free 'editorial'. The entitlement is for up to 600 words per page of advertising, and pro rata for other sizes of advertisement. The advertiser supplies the copy for the 'editorial'.

## THE SOLICITOR'S JOURNAL: CHARITY APPEALS SUPPLEMENT

Oyez Longman Publishing, 21–27 Lamb's Conduit Street, London WC1N 3NJ
*Telephone: 01-242 2548*

**Publication date:** end-November.

**Format:** 297mm × 210mm (A4); magazine format (wire stitched). Type area: 261mm × 183mm.

**Readership:** free to subscribers of The Solicitor's Journal, a weekly magazine for the legal profession with a circulation of 6,886.

**Cost:** Full-page £275; $\frac{1}{2}$-page £150; $\frac{1}{4}$-page £90.

The Charity Appeals Supplement consists of advertising by charities and a review of the law affecting charities during the previous twelve months. There is an alphabetical listing of charities with up to 250 words of 'editorial' matter supplied by the charities themselves.

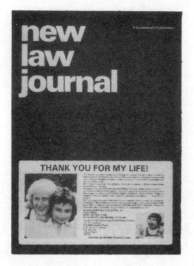

## NEW LAW JOURNAL ANNUAL CHARITIES REVIEW

T. G. Scott & Son,
30–32 Southampton Street,
London WC2 7HR
(advertising contractor)
*Telephone: 01–240 2032*

**Publication date:** end-April.

**Format:** 247mm × 185mm;
magazine format (wire stitched).
Type area: 197mm × 140mm.

**Readership:** Free to subscribers to
the New Law Journal, a weekly
magazine for the legal profession
with a circulation of 8,616. The
print run of the Supplement is
9,500.

**Cost:** Full-page £154; ½-page £80;
¼-page £47; ⅛-page £25.

The *Annual Charities Review* (which is
published by Butterworths) consists of
paid advertisements with short articles
on charity law at the beginning, and an
index and digest of advertisers at the
end which includes details of the
advertisers supplied by themselves (up
to 300 words). All advertisers are entitled to this free 'editorial' entry.

## NEW LAW JOURNAL CHRISTMAS APPEALS SUPPLEMENT

T. G. Scott & Son,
30–32 Southampton Street,
London WC2E 7HR
*Telephone: 01–240 2032*

**Publication date:** end-November.

**Format:** 297mm × 210mm (A4);
magazine format (wire stitched).
Type area: 255mm × 185mm.

**Readership:** Free to subscribers of
the New Law Journal, a weekly
magazine.

**Cost:** Full-page £230; ½-page £135;
¼-page £85; ⅛-page £56.

The Christmas Appeals Supplement
consists solely of paid advertisements
from charities. It is published in a
slightly larger format than the Annual
Charities Review. The publisher is
Butterworths.

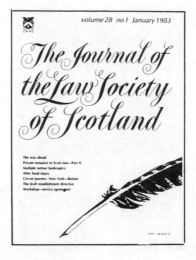

## THE SCOTS LAW TIMES: CHRISTMAS CHARITY SUPPLEMENT

W. Green & Son Ltd.,
St. Giles Street, Edinburgh EH1 1PU
*Telephone: 031–225 4879*

**Publication date:** last Friday in November.

**Format:** 263mm × 189mm; magazine format (wire stitched). Type area: 235mm × 159mm.

**Readership:** free distribution with the Scots Law Times, which is a weekly newspaper for the Scottish legal profession with an approximate circulation of 2,000.

**Cost:** Full-page £73; ½-page £48; ¼-page £30.

This is the only charity supplement published by a Scottish law journal. The cost of the advertisement also includes a free listing with approximately 200 words of 'editorial' matter supplied by the charity.

## THE JOURNAL OF THE LAW SOCIETY OF SCOTLAND

Charlotte Publicity Service,
44A Melville Street,
Edinburgh EH3 7HF
(advertising contractor)
*Telephone: 031–226 7310
and 031–225 8634*

**Publication date:** monthly.

**Format:** 297mm × 210mm (A4); magazine format (wire stitched). Type area: 260mm × 177mm.

**Readership:** Every practising solicitor in Scotland receives a copy as part of their membership of the Law Society of Scotland. Circulation is approximately 7,000.

**Cost:** Full-page £136; ½-page £79; ¼-page £50 (charity rates).

The Journal does not produce a special charity advertising supplement, but charities can and do advertise in the normal monthly edition of the Journal.

## THE SCOTTISH LAW GAZETTE

PUBLISHED FOR CIRCULATION AMONGST MEMBERS BY THE COUNCIL OF THE SCOTTISH LAW AGENTS SOCIETY

Vol. 51, No. 1
MARCH 1983

### THE SCOTTISH LAW GAZETTE

Charlotte Publicity Service,
44A Melville Street,
Edinburgh EH3 7HF
(advertising contractor)
*Telephone: 031–226 7310
and 031–225 8634*

**Publication date:** quarterly.

**Format:** 250mm × 185mm; magazine format. Type area: 210mm × 160mm.

**Readership:** The legal profession in Scotland. Circulation is approximately 2,500.

**Cost:** Full-page £75; ½-page £41; ¼-page £24 (no discounts are available to charities on these prices).

The Gazette does not produce a special charity advertising supplement but charities can advertise in the normal quarterly edition of the Gazette which is published in March, June, September and December of each year.

### THE BANKER

Minister House, Arthur Street,
London EC4R 9AX
*Telephone: 01–254 6251*

**Format:** 267mm × 203mm; magazine. Type area: 230mm × 165mm.

**Cost:** Full-page £850; ½-page £450; ¼-page £225.

Published monthly for the banking profession: it has a circulation of 11,227. No special advertising supplement for charities.

### BANKER'S MAGAZINE

Waterlow Publishers, Maxwell House,
74 Worship Street, London ECZA ZEN
*Telephone: 01–377 4600*

**Format:** 297mm × 210mm (A4); magazine. Type area 270mm × 185mm.

**Cost:** Full-page £540; ½-page £270; ¼-page £135; ⅛-page £67.50.

Published monthly for the banking profession: it has a circulation of 12,129. No special advertising supplement for charities.

## SUMMARY OF DETAILS

| | Publication date | Circu-lation | Size | Format | Cost per page |
|---|---|---|---|---|---|
| Will to Charity: June | June | 10,000* | A5 | paperback | £485 |
| Will to Charity: November | November | 10,000* | A5 | paperback | £142 per ½-column |
| Charities Digest | November | 6,000* | 210 × 129 | paperback | £130 and £3 per column inch** |
| Law Society's Gazette | November | over 40,000 | A4 | perfect-bound | £700 |
| New Law Journal: April | April | 8,616 | 247 × 185 | magazine | £154 |
| New Law Journal: November | November | 8,616 | A4 | magazine | £230 |
| Solicitor's Journal | November | 6,886 | A4 | magazine | £275 |
| Scots Law Times | November | 2,000* | 273 × 187 | magazine | £73 |
| Journal of Law Society of Scotland | monthly*** | 7,000* | A4 | magazine | £136 |
| Scottish Law Gazette | quarterly*** | 2,500* | 250 × 185 | magazine | £75 |
| The Banker | monthly*** | 11,227 | 267 × 203 | magazine | £850 |
| Banker's Magazine | monthly*** | 12,129 | A4 | magazine | £540 |

&ast; Publisher's estimate.
&ast;&ast; Plus VAT.
&ast;&ast;&ast; No special advertising supplement published. Details given are for advertising in the main publication.
A5 = 210mm × 148mm; A4 = 297mm × 210mm

# Highlighting the memorial aspect

by Asher Corren, Executive Director,
Nightingale House

I want to look at raising money through providing memorials. In one sense this has nothing at all to do with getting legacies. In another it is quite similar. It is to do with fund-raising at death, and with perpetuating a memory through giving money to charity – although with memorials it is someone else's memory not your own.

Nightingale House was founded in 1840. It provides residential accommodation and nursing care for elderly Jewish people. Once we accept an old person, she (or he) can stay with us until she dies. The average age of our residents is 88, and this has been increasing in recent years with the rise in life expectancy of the population generally. We have 400 beds and we plan to increase this in our current capital programme to 450. We do not expect to expand beyond that level. We are the largest home for the elderly in the country. And we are well established within the Jewish community, which is important to us in our fund-raising. A large part of our income comes in the form of grants and fees from the statutory authorities. As we are not a housing association for the elderly, we do not get our capital requirements from any statutory body. We need to fund-raise to meet our capital needs, to furnish the new facilities we provide and to top up our running costs. We use all manner of fund-raising methods, including getting legacy income. The aspect of our fund-raising which I would like to discuss here is raising money through memorials.

Fund-raising through memorials is a method of fund-raising which is used successfully by the Jewish community. But it is also something that has been used by other denominations and by non-denominational charities (such as theatres in the naming of seats). What we do is based in part upon the opportunities available to us through the particular nature of Jewish observance and culture. Although what we can do will be different from what others can do, in essence it will be the same and the lessons to be learned are of general interest.

Fund-raising through memorials can be very controversial because this is a very sensitive matter, especially at the time of bereavement. However, the majority of people would wish to perpetuate the memory of their dear ones and, at the same time, help a charity which they have supported for many years. This has to be handled very carefully and on a personal level, certainly not through correspondence.

I would like to look at some of the ways in which we can raise funds from memorials:

## 1. Memorial Prayers

There is an ancient Jewish tradition for surviving parents or children to say prayers every year on the anniversary of the death. This prayer is known as 'Kaddish' and it requires the mourner to pray in the Synagogue. The mourner does not always have the time (or inclination) to do this himself, or he may be at a meeting or abroad or ill. He wants to ensure that the prayer is at least said by someone (even when he may also say it as well) and for ever if possible.

We have a Synagogue at Nightingale House, where the elderly people will say 'Kaddish' on behalf of the mourner. They feel that this is doing something useful for someone else. It is also a means of raising money, although of course we do not, nor would we wish to, charge the mourner for doing this.

What we do is to inscribe the name of the deceased on a memorial board in the Synagogue and the Kaddish prayers are recited on the anniversary of death each year and for as long as Nightingale House exists. We make a charge for the inscription itself, but not for saying the prayers. We tell people specifically that they do not have to pay us for that, but we do intimate that if they care to give us a donation it will be gratefully received. Most do.

We raise a lot of money in this way. We publicise this service throughout the Jewish community. And we feel that we do something useful within the Jewish tradition which at the same time helps the Home financially.

## 2. Naming seats and rooms

We try to encourage people to donate to our Charity and they may wish to do this in return for a memorial. We can provide this service. It matches the needs of the donor and recipient. In a way it is selling a product, but via this method we are able to raise a considerable amount of money.

**Synagogue seats:** we can inscribe the name of a person on a Synagogue seat in perpetuity.

**Beds:** we have 400 beds, soon to be 450. We can name all of them, but without actually putting the name on the bed. We have a 'naming of beds board' on which the name of the person is inscribed. We encounter almost no problems with the fact that there is not a plaque on the bed itself.

**Furniture:** we have decided that we do not want to have plaques all around an elderly person's bedroom. This would give an impression almost of living in a cemetery, which is not very pleasant for the resident. So again we have a naming board for those who have bought furniture for a bedroom.

**Equipment:** here we can put a plaque on the equipment, without any problems, should people wish this. We can name physiotherapy equipment, X-ray equipment or whatever. It does no harm and it will barely be noticed by the residents.

**Bedrooms:** we name a room for a great deal of money, because we need the money to build the room. We do put up a plaque on the door, but we compromise by ensuring that the plaque is not too large.

**Public rooms:** provided we have a potential donor and can agree a sum, we will name a public room, a TV lounge, a dining room, a servery, a pantry, a wing of a building, or whatever. We feel that what we are doing is worthwhile; we provide a good service in looking after the elderly within our community. And naming a room is a device to raise a very substantial sum of money from individual donors or Trusts, etc.

**Garden seats:** we name seats in the garden. This is a type of memorial which I particularly like. In one of the parks near my house I often sit on a bench inscribed *'In memory of Gladys, who* *died aged 97, who enjoyed the view from this bench for 77 years'*. I enjoy the view too, and I can benefit because someone has commemorated this dear friend, Gladys.

In our Annual Report we have a 'price list' for naming:

To name a bedroom costs £5,000;

To name a bed costs £1,000;

To furnish a room costs £500;

To name a seat costs £150.

Because we are well established within the Jewish community – many have heard of us, others have had a relative living with us – this is solely where we direct our fund-raising. We arrange a lot of meetings within the Jewish community. We talk to Rabbis. We contact solicitors, either by writing a personal letter or by telephoning. We ask our friends to tell their friends – and their friends may be solicitors, doctors, accountants and others who are listened to for their professional advice. A good word about you from the right person at the right time can do an incalculable amount of good.

In raising capital sums through memorials, we also encourage our donors to give in a tax-effective way. A covenant increases the value of the gift by the tax we can reclaim, and donors with high incomes can benefit as well through the Higher Rate Relief that they can obtain. We are able today to accept covenants for 4, 7 or even 10 years. The increased income more than offsets the fact that we do not get a large sum all at once. Indeed through the device of a 'Loan-Covenant' you can obtain the tax advantages of a covenanted donation whilst receiving the lump sum payment immediately.

We have to administer all this activity, and this includes getting legacy income too. We need to handle the correspondence, organise our publicity, meet people, etc. A legacy of £10,000 would pay for all this. Naturally we hope for a great deal more, and generally we are not disappointed.

Fund-raising through memorials is a 'difficult' activity. You need first to acknowledge that as much as death is sad, it is possible to raise money because of it. I think this is realistic. You cannot escape from the fact that people do die, and that those who survive may want to perpetuate the memory of a dear one. It is not an area of fund-raising that you should rush headlong into. It is a very sensitive area and you need to take a great deal of care. You have to respect the feelings and the wishes of your donors, who are giving under difficult circumstances. You need to work hard, but the financial rewards can be substantial.

# PART III

# ADMINISTRATION AND TAXATION MATTERS

# Some basic definitions

Let us begin by looking at the main aspects of a Will and its administration. This will define a few basic terms which are commonly used in the context of drawing up and administering Wills.

## A Will

A Will is the legal document which determines how the possessions of a person shall be distributed on his death (after deduction of any debts, funeral expenses, legal costs and any Capital Transfer Tax that may be payable). A person making a Will is known as a 'testator' or occasionally a 'legator'. The Will is binding on the administrators of the estate who must distribute the assets of the estate in the manner specified in the Will – but subject to the rights that any family and dependants may have through the *1975 Inheritance (Provision for Family and Dependants) Act*, where the Court may order some or all of the estate to be distributed to the testator's family and dependants (*see Appendix 2*). A Will need not be drawn up by a solicitor, nor need it be witnessed by a solicitor. But because a Will determines precisely the distribution of the assets of the estate, any errors in drafting or ambiguities in its content can cause serious problems when the estate comes to be divided up. So whether or not people seek legal help in drafting their Will, it is a job which does not need to be done well. The people benefiting from the Will are known as the 'beneficiaries' or 'legatees'. The gift of an asset or item of property, is known as a 'specific bequest', or if realty (that is land or property), a 'specific devise'. A gift of a cash sum is referred to as a 'pecuniary legacy'.

## Executing a Will

It is important not only that a Will clearly reflects the Testator's intentions, but also that it is effective. To be valid a Will must be properly executed. The procedure is laid down in the *1837 Wills Act*. . . *'No Will shall be valid unless it shall be in writing and executed in the manner hereinafter mentioned*. . . *it shall be signed at the foot or end thereof by the Testator, or by some other person in his presence and by his direction; and such signature shall be made or acknowledged by the Testator in the presence of two or more witnesses at the same time, and such witnesses shall attest and shall subscribe the Will in the presence of the Testator, but no form of attestation shall be necessary.'* Although no form of attestation is necessary, where there is none or where it is insufficiently worded this can cause problems when the Will comes to be proved, and it is best that the Will does contain some form of attestation which might be as simple as *'Signed by the above-named in our joint presence and then by us in his (hers)'*. Following the signature of the Will by the testator in the presence of the witnesses, both witnesses should sign before any of them leave the room. Through this simple procedure the requirements should be met. Certain people are barred from being a witness of a Will, in particular the testator's spouse or any beneficiary of the Will. Normally the procedures for signing and attesting a Will are well understood and there should be no problems. But where the testator is ill or mentally ill problems can arise and proper legal advice is best sought in such circumstances.

## Changing a Will

A Will reflects the testator's intentions at the time he makes the Will. His intentions may change as may his circumstances, and it is wise to review the provisions of a Will from time to time. It may be that the testator wishes to make changes to his Will, and he can do this in two ways – either by drawing up a new Will or by adding a 'Codicil' to his existing Will. A Codicil is a supplement to a Will and is a legal document which has to be executed in exactly the same way as the original Will. A Codicil can be used to revoke certain provisions in a Will, to alter others or to add new provisions. Codicils are best used only where there are straightforward alterations to the terms of the Will. In other circumstances it is best to make a new Will. There is no limit to the number of Codicils that can be made. The way an estate is distributed is in accordance with the Will *and all Codicils to it*. A testator wishing to alter a Will should not in any circumstances try to amend his existing Will. Any alterations, additions or deletions to an existing Will are presumed to have been made after the signing of the Will and are therefore invalid (unless the contrary can be proved), and any legacy appearing underneath the signature is not valid either. A new Will does not automatically replace an existing Will. A previous Will can be revoked in one of two ways – either the new Will will contain a 'revocation clause' which revokes the previous Will or all previous Wills made by the testator, or the testator destroys the Will *with the intention of revoking it* either himself or by causing someone else to do it in his presence. It is best if the new Will contains a revocation clause and the previous Will is destroyed, which avoids the eventuality of the earlier Will being discovered and not the subsequent one at the time of the testator's death. Marriage by the testator will automatically revoke any valid Will unless that Will has clearly anticipated the possibility of the testator's marriage. So on marriage a new Will needs to be drawn up, and this is particularly important because the intestacy rules (see below) may not reflect the wishes of the testator. Divorce, on the other hand, does not affect the validity of a Will.

## Intestacy

When a person dies without leaving a Will he is said to have died 'intestate'. In such circumstances his property is divided up according to a formula contained in the *1925 Administration of Estates Act*. The provisions of this Act are quite complicated but can broadly be summarised as follows: All personal effects, furniture, cars go to the surviving spouse. Where the remainder of the estate is worth less than £40,000 the whole of the estate goes to the surviving spouse; where it is worth more than £40,000 then £40,000 goes to the spouse; one half of the remainder is divided amongst the children and the remainder is held in trust for the children with the spouse getting a life interest. If there are children but no surviving spouse the children get the whole of the estate. If there is a surviving spouse but no children, the spouse gets the personal effects etc., the next £85,000 and half the rest with the remainder going to the deceased's parents. Where the deceased was not married the estate passes to his parents, and failing that to his siblings, failing that to his grandparents, and failing that to the descendants of his grandparents. If there is nobody to inherit the property, the estate reverts to the Crown.

## Executors

The people responsible for dealing with the estate are known as 'personal representatives'. Where they are appointed by the testator under the terms of the Will they are known as 'executors'. The executors are responsible for seeing that the estate is distributed in accordance with the testator's wishes on his death and for ensuring that the statutory procedures for administering the Will are undertaken and that any tax that is due is paid. A valid Will requires at least one executor, but many have more than one. Where a person dies intestate, the personal representatives are known as 'administrators'. An executor may also be a beneficiary under the Will.

## Probate

A 'Grant of Probate', often referred to as 'probate', is the official document from the High Court providing the executors with the written legal authority to deal with the property of the estate. A Grant of Probate is necessary where property has to be disposed of or sold, the contents of a bank account released to the executors, or the rights of certain assets such as pension arrears established. A Grant of Probate may not be necessary where an estate consists only of cash, certain National Savings certificates and personal effects. Where a person dies intestate, the administrators of the estate are granted 'Letters of Administration'. A Grant of Probate or Letters of Administration are only given to the personal representative on settlement of the estimated liability of the estate to Capital Transfer Tax.

## Capital Transfer Tax (CTT)

Capital Transfer Tax is the capital tax levied on property passing on death. It is a progressive tax rising to a maximum of 75 per cent. The rate of tax payable depends on the value of the estate, the amount of exempt transfers (the main exemptions are for transfers to a surviving spouse, to charities and to political parties) and the amount given by the testator in the form of chargeable transfers in the last ten years of the deceased's life. Full details of the way Capital Transfer Tax operates are given in Appendix 1.

# SOME BASIC DEFINITIONS

## The Administration of the Will

Administration of the Will consists of several functions; the executors (or administrators) have to prove their right to handle the estate through obtaining a Grant of Probate; the estate has to be divided amongst any creditors existing at the time of death and the beneficiaries of the Will; and Capital Transfer Tax, legal expenses and funeral expenses have to be paid. The main functions involved in the administration of the Will are:

(a) Establishing the nature and the value of all the assets belonging to the deceased.

(b) Establishing what debts (if any) were owed by the deceased at the date of his death.

(c) Working out an estimate of the Capital Transfer Tax that is payable. This will be based on the net value of the estate (the gross value less any liabilities) and the amount of the estate which is to be transferred to exempt beneficiaries.

(d) Preparing the official documents required by the Inland Revenue and Probate Registry.

(e) Paying Capital Transfer Tax.

(f) Receiving a grant of probate (or letters of administration).

(g) Selling any property which needs to be disposed of to pay any debts or any legacies under the terms of the Will.

(h) Paying legacies and handing over specific bequests in strict accordance with the terms of the Will.

(i) Handing over any property which is to be held in trust to trustees appointed under the terms of the Will.

(j) Paying any legal fees and preparing the accounts of the estate.

(k) Distributing the residue of the estate to the residuary beneficiaries.

The complexity of administration of a Will will depend on the contents of the estate and how they are to be distributed. It may be a simple matter to identify and value all the assets comprised in the estate and to determine what amounts were owing at the time of death, or it may be extremely complicated. The estate may be handed over lock, stock and barrel to a surviving spouse, or the assets may have to be converted into cash. The beneficiaries may all be to hand, or they may need to be traced. The executor's function lasts from the date of death until the assets have been distributed according to the terms of the Will. The executors may handle all the administration themselves or they may seek professional help (usually from a firm of solicitors).

## The beneficiaries of the Will

Those people receiving gifts of cash or property under a Will are known as the 'beneficiaries'. In the case of the gift of a specific asset or item of property the gift is known as a 'bequest'. In the case of a cash sum or a share of the estate after all other gifts have been made, the gift is known as a 'legacy', and the recipient is known as a 'legatee'. Some of the ways in which the testator may dispose of his property are:

(a) **A pecuniary legacy:** This is the gift of a specific sum of money which is mentioned in the Will. One problem is that the real value of the sum may decline over the period from when the Will was made until the testators death, and the purchasing power of the money eventually received by the beneficiary represents only a fraction of what may have been originally intended. So unless a Codicil is added increasing the amount of a pecuniary legacy, the legatee may derive rather less benefit that was intended by the testator when he drew up the Will.

(b) **A specific bequest:** This is the gift of an identifiable asset. *'I bequeath my shares in ICI, my house, my home computer etc. . . .'* The asset has to be described so that it can be identified without any doubt. Should the asset that has been bequeathed no longer belong to the testator at the time of death – it may have been sold, lost or thrown away – the intended beneficiary will receive nothing. The executors are not empowered to make an equivalent gift in lieu.

(c) **A residuary legacy:** After making a number of pecuniary legacies and specific bequests, the testator may give the residue of the estate to one or several named beneficiaries. This is known as a residuary legacy. Where there is only one residuary beneficiary he is known as a 'sole residuary legatee', and where there are several they are known as 'joint residuary legatees'. Should the estate be insufficient to cover the specific bequests and pecuniary legacies and any Capital Transfer Tax that may be payable, there will be no residue and the residuary legatees will receive nothing. Except as directed otherwise in the Will, any Capital Transfer Tax that is payable will be paid out of the residue of the Estate before distribution. A residuary beneficiary is entitled to a copy of a Will and to a copy of the final accounts which detail how the assets of the estate have been distributed.

(d) **A life interest:** Where a life interest is granted the beneficiary of that interest known as a 'life tenant' receives income from the specified property during his lifetime. On his death the capital is distributed as directed in the Will.

(e) **A reversionary legacy:** After a life interest has been enjoyed by the life tenant the assets are distributed. The beneficiary is known as a 'reversionary legatee' or 'remainderman'. During the life tenancy the assets are administered by trustees who must attempt to draw a fair balance between the interests of the life tenant who requires a fair income and the interests of the reversionary legatee who requires the capital value of the assets to be maintained in so far as is possible.

(f) **A conditional bequest:** A Charity is often named in a Will as a long stop, should all else fail. *'I leave my estate to my wife, or failing that to be divided amongst my children'*. This is all right except when the wife predeceases the testator and there are no surviving children. So a clause may be added that failing all else the estate shall be distributed to a named charity. Because charities exist (or are deemed to do so) in perpetuity, a charity may be named as residuary legatee in these cirumstances. It is unlikely that the charity will receive anything under this sort of Will. It is a protection to the testator against dying intestate. And it may just be that all else will fail and that the charity will receive the bequest.

(g) **A grave interest:** One particular form of conditional bequest is where there is a trust for the erection and maintenance of a grave of the deceased (or some other person). The maintenance of a grave can be done so long as there are adequate funds for the task, or so long as the grave actually exists. The Will should make provision for the distribution of the capital at a time when it is no longer possible to expend the income of the trust on maintaining the grave.

(h) **Family and Dependants:** Under the *1975 Inheritance (Provision for Family and Dependants) Act*, certain members of the deceased's family or other people being maintained by the deceased immediately prior to his death may have a right to receive some or all of the estate. This right can be established on application to the Court, and the amount that any person can receive is decided by the Court or by agreement with the residuary beneficiaries. For fuller details of the provisions of the Act see Appendix 2.

# Will draftsmanship

Charitable benefaction is small when compared with the value of all assets passing on death – small in number, as many people make no charitable gifts at all; and small in amount. Occasionally a charity will be left the residue of an estate, or a share of it, and in some cases this can amount to a very large amount indeed. Although legacies are an important source of income for charities, charitable giving on death is of far less importance to donors.

So the main job for charities is to try to influence people to leave more money to charity and to influence more people to leave money to charity. Charities need to understand how Wills are made, and how the draftsman of a Will can be assisted so that the intended legacy does pass eventually to the charity without problem.

Most people seek professional advice when making a Will, although some try to do it themselves. It may be very laudable to write your own Will, and you certainly avoid legal fees if doing it this way. But a badly written Will can be worse than no Will at all. At least with no Will the laws of intestacy will apply. With a badly written Will the only people who benefit are lawyers when they try to sort things out when the estate comes to be distributed – and this is the one 'beneficiary' the testator tried to avoid benefiting when he decided to write his own Will.

There are a number of good guides on Will writing (*see Resources section at the end of the book*). And if their advice is closely followed and the terms of the Will are relatively simple, then things will probably be fine. Just to give an example of how things might go wrong. A testator states in his Will that *'I leave all my worldly goods to my wife.'* This seems simple, right and proper, and it avoids Capital Transfer Tax. But his wife dies before he does and he is so distressed that he forgets to make another Will. The laws of intestacy will apply, but he has no children. So it is almost certain that the estate will be distributed in a way he would not have wished. So a Will does need to be clearly and unambiguously drafted, it needs to cover foreseeable contingencies, and it has to be properly executed.

If professional advice is sought, there is of course no guarantee that there will not be problems. But problems are far less likely to occur when someone with experience of writing Wills assists with their drafting. The most usual source of help for Will drafting is a solicitor. In recent years the clearing banks have also become involved. They see this as being part of a family financial service and as a new source of business. There has been some controversy between the banks and the Law Society (the solicitors' professional body) as to how far the banks have become involved, but their involvement is on the increase. Another potential source of advice is an accountant. But at the present time there appears to be no widespread involvement of accountants in Will drafting.

When a person makes a Will he will consider his assets and his approximate net worth and whom he wishes to benefit. Among the beneficiaries he may wish to give some money to charity. He can do this in one of several ways:

(a) He may have specific charities in mind that he wishes to benefit. There may be charities he has had some connection with or which for some particular reason he wishes to benefit. Or he may want to give money for a particular cause and the 'brand name' charity springs to mind – cancer (Imperial Cancer Research, Cancer Research Campaign); the elderly (Help the Aged, Age Concern); children (Save the Children, Barnardo's); animals (RSPCA); etc.

(b) He may wish to benefit charity in general, or particular types of charity, and seek advice from his advisor as to which particular charities he should benefit. There is no evidence that solicitors have any particular expertise in judging the merits of one charity as against another. But it is a fact of life that they are called on to give advice from time to time and do so. And charities in consequence direct some advertising effort at making their existence known to solicitors and convincing them of the worthiness of their cause. How much discretion or influence the solicitor has at the drafting stage is not wholly clear. There may be a tendency for solicitors to deny that they have any influence at all, but the results of charity advertising do indicate otherwise.

(c) He may wish to set aside a specific sum for the benefit of charities in general or particular types of charity, and leave it to his executors to distribute the money as they see fit.

Having decided to leave money to charity, one thing that causes problems is the inaccurate description of the particular charities that are to benefit. Quite often the charity is given a very loose name; sometimes it is completely wrong. Not enough attention has been focussed on how important it is for the draftsman of the Will to get the name right in the Will. A lot of solicitors simply accept without checking what the testator says. And then problems arise when it is too late to put things right – on the testator's death.

It is best that a charity is given its proper name in full, its address (which will help when the executors need to contact it when the estate is being administered), and in England and Wales its charity registration number. This identifies the charity beyond any doubt. Charities in their advertising should show these basic details – and not all do so. And they should hope that the solicitor turns to one of the directories or charity advertising supplements produced for lawyers when he tries to verify the information given to him by the testator. These are probably the only sources of information readily available to solicitors, as they are unlikely to check the primary source, the Official Register of Charities, kept by the Charity Commission in London and Liverpool.

On occasion it is found that a gift has been made to a non-existent institution. This may be because the charity has ceased to exist, but more likely it is because nobody bothered to check the details at the time the Will was drawn up. If a gift were made to a non-existent individual, such a gift would lapse, (for example, where the beneficiary had pre-deceased the testator). There would be nobody to give the legacy to. A gift to a non-existent charity does not necessarily lapse. In such circumstances it is necessary to enquire into the prime object of the testator's bounty – what did he really wish to do? Did he intend to benefit the named institution itself or more generally benefit the purpose of the institution? If the gift were intended specifically for the named charity it would probably lapse; if it were intended for that general charitable purpose, it would probably then be applied to another institution for similar purposes.

So if the charity has a registered number and the solicitor is aware of this and includes it in the Will, then it is:

(a) Obvious that the intended organisation is a charity. So provided that the gift is made to that charity for a charitable purpose (and not for a specific purpose which is not fact charitable) there will be no problem.

(b) Obvious precisely which charity will benefit, and this will avoid all dispute later on.

At this stage let us consider the definition of a charity. What is deemed to be charitable is a matter for the Courts to decide; and in England and Wales the Charity Commission (in consultation with the Inland Revenue, who are responsible for granting the tax concessions to charities) in the light of established case law will decide whether an organisation is a charity and should be entered on to the Register of Charities. What is charitable and what is not charitable stems from a preamble to the Statutute of Elizabeth I in 1601:

> 'Whereas landes tenementes rentes annuities pfittes hereditamentes, goodes chattels money and stockes of money, have bene heretofore given limitted appointed and assigned, as well by the Queenes moste excellent Majestie and her moste noble progenitors, as by sondrie other well disposed psons, some for releife of aged impotent and poore people, some for maintenance of sicke and maymed souldiers and marriners, schooles of learninge, free schooles and schollers in univsities, some for repaire of bridges portes havens causwaies churches seabankes and highewaies, some for educacon and pfermente of orphans, some for or towardes reliefe stocke or maintenance for howses of correccon, some for mariages of poore maides, some for supportacon ayde and helpe of younge tradesmen, handiecraftesmen, and psons decayed, and others for releife or redemption of prisoners or captives, and for aide or ease of any poore inhabitantes concerninge paymente of fifteenes, setting out of souldiers and other taxes; wiche landes tenements rents annuities pfitts hereditaments goodes chattells money and stockes of money nevtheles have not byn imployed acordinge to the charitable intente of the givers and founders thereof, by reason of fraudes breaches of truste and negligence in those that shoulde pay delyver and imploy the same'

Many of the items listed as being charitable in this preamble had been previously listed in *'Piers Ploughman'*. From this beginning the definition of what is charitable has been continually elaborated by case law up until the present day. In 1891 Lord Macnaghten tried to clarify the situation, and he defined four main 'heads of charity' (areas of activity which are held to be charitable); these can be further subdivided as follows:

1. Relief of poverty
2. Advancement of education (including research and the arts)
3. Advancement of religion
4. Promotion of health (including care and relief of the aged and the disabled)
5. Social rehabilitation (for refugees, victims of disaster, ex-prisoners, addicts, etc.)
6. Provision and maintenance of public amenities (recreation facilities, libraries, museums, parks, historic monuments, etc.)
7. Protection of animals, birds and the natural environment
8. Other purposes beneficial to the community.

In addition to the activity falling within one or more of the heads of charity, two further conditions need to be met: (a) the purpose of the gift must be wholly charitable; it is no good if some of the gift can be applied to a non-charitable purpose. And (b) there must be public benefit, where 'public' means a sufficiently wide section of the community. A gift which is not for public benefit is not charitable. This may occur where the beneficiaries are too restricted as a group (as in the Penlee Lifeboat Disaster Fund or with company funded education schemes for the children of their employees) or where there is deemed to be no public benefit at all.

Having dealt with the definition of charity, some problems can arise where a testator wishes to leave a legacy for purposes which he thinks are charitable, but which turn out not to be charitable. Let us look at some instances of how this might happen.

## 1. The named institution is not a charity

It is quite a common occurrence that a testator wants to leave money to an institution which is not in fact a charity – for example, a professional association where benefit is restricted to members of that association. If the gift is made in terms that make it a charitable gift but to a non-charitable institution, the gift may fail. Under charity law a charity is assumed to have perpetual status and the Court has ultimate control over the gift. With a non-charitable institution this will not be the case, and depending on the rules of the association, the gift may not be valid.

## 2. The money is left for a purpose which is not charitable

A common instance of where money is left for a purpose which is not charitable – and where the testator believes that it has been left for a charitable purpose – is for the erection and keeping in good repair of a tomb, monument or gravestone, for himself or for someone else. *'The grave's a fine and private place'* said Marvell, but there is no element of public benefit in providing it. In 1981 it was held that the erection of a monument for Earl Mountbatten was in fact a charitable purpose because of the esteem in which he was held by the public – in this instance a person of national significance was being commemorated, and the memorial was likely to foster patriotism and good citizenship. But for more humble mortals such a gift would not be charitable.

## 3. The gift is made to a charity but for purposes which are not charitable

It is not enough that a gift is made to a charity. The *purposes* of the gift need to be charitable too. If the money is given to a charity but tied to a specific purpose which is not charitable, then it will not be a charitable gift. A common instance is where money is given to an animal charity for the benefit of the deceased's own animal – *'to the Barking Cats Home to provide comfort and company for my cat Tabitha for the remainder of her life'*. A gift for the benefit of a particular animal is not a charitable gift, although where the benefit is for animals in general it would be. Another instance is where although the gift is made to a charity, it is tied to the provision of a personal memorial for the donor. The testator has to be careful not to impose a binding obligation on the trustees to apply the money to this non-charitable purpose (the provision of a personal memorial). However, by careful drafting it is possible to make an outright gift to the charity, which is a charitable gift, and to give the trustees of the charity the discretion to provide the memorial.

## 4. There is no general charitable intention

The purposes of the gift need to be wholly charitable and there must be no possibility that the gift could be expended for a non-charitable purpose. If money is given '*to trustees upon trust for the charity*', it is most important that the application of the funds to charity is obligatory. Sloppy drafting can lead to problems. If the trustees are permitted some alternative application the gift will turn out not to be charitable. This often happens for example where a residue is left to trustees '*for such objects of benevolence and liberality as the trustees in their discretion think fit*'. Benevolence and liberality is far wider than charity in its strict legal sense. This is just the sort of case where a solicitor may have told the testator that the gift is charitable and where it is not. There is no obligation to devote all or any of the funds to charity. Indeed the whole gift may well be void for uncertainty.

The two main legal problems encountered when money is left to charity are that the named charity is not identifiable and that the charitable gift is made for purposes which are not in fact charitable. Great care needs to be taken in naming the institution correctly, in ensuring that it is in fact a charity, and in drafting the Will properly so that the gift does not fail. Legacies are a very technical area of the law. It is very sad when the intentions of the testator are frustrated because a mistake has been made, and as a result the money goes elsewhere than where it was intended.

These problems are caused entirely at the drafting stage, but they do not surface until after the death of the testator when the Will has been probated. It is the duty of the Executors to pay the money to the beneficiaries in strict accordance with the terms of the Will. They have no discretionary powers unless these are specifically stated in the Will. If the provisions of the Will are uncertain or cannot be complied with, then the Executors may need to take legal advice or go to Court to get a precise ruling as to how they should dispose of the estate. If the estate is not distributed in strict accordance with the terms of the Will, the distribution can be challenged. This is why it is important for the Executors to get it right, and doubly important for the testator to state his intentions clearly, unambiguously and using a correct form of words. Where a testator wishes to leave any sizeable amount to charity he should make extra sure that there are no legal or technical pitfalls − otherwise he may fail to benefit the charities of his choice, and the mistakes will involve that much more money.

There is one other problem which affects charities in receipt of a legacy. In most cases a charity will be left money to spend on its charitable work as it wishes. Occasionally the testator will have attached a condition to the bequest. This condition may cause no problems to the charity – the testator may wish the money to be spent on one particular aspect of the charity's work, or that it be applied to a capital project or added to the charity's permanent endowment. On the other hand, the condition attached to the gift may be unacceptable to the charity.

Where the conditions attached to the bequest are unacceptable the charity is, of course, free to refuse the money. But it may be possible to get a Court ruling that the conditions be dropped. To do this the Court will have to decide whether the condition was an essential part of the primary object of the gift or whether it was not. And if it was not, the Court can determine that the gift can be made without the unacceptable condition. This principle is illustrated by a ruling that the Royal College of Surgeons obtained in 1965. The testatrix in her Will stated that she had long wished to found medical studentships, and she bequeathed a sum of £5,000 for that purpose – but with the condition that the students to be eligible had to be British born and not of the Roman Catholic or Jewish faith. This condition was found not to be an essential part of the gift, rather that the testatrix had had an overriding general charitable intention to found the studentships. So the College was able to found the studentships without including any element of religious discrimination. And the same principle would apply where the conditions of the gift were illegal or contrary to public policy – if there were a general charitable intention then the gift could be made without the condition; and if there were not, it would fail.

It may also be impossible or impracticable for the charity to accept a legacy for the particular purpose that it was given for. Again the same principle will apply – the Court would have to decide whether the condition was or was not subsidiary to the main charitable purpose of the gift.

Where money is left in trust for a charity subject to a life interest and between the time of the testator's death and the time when the gift becomes available for distribution to the charity the condition attached to the gift may have become impossible and impracticable to be put into effect, then the following will apply. Where the terms of the gift are so specific as to exclude any general charitable intention other than the specific charitable purpose of the gift, then the gift will fail. In all other circumstances it will be held that the money has been effectively dedicated to charity at the time of the testator's death and that it should be applied to charity on the *cy près* principle – that is as nearly as possible in accordance with the original intention if that intention is incapable of being carried out. An example of this is where money was bequeathed subject to a life interest to be applied to mission work in the district served by a particular Methodist Church. When the money became available, the church and much of the neighbourhood had been demolished and it was impracticable that the intended mission work be carried out. In this case the Court directed how the money should be applied.

*(This section was prepared with the assistance of Richard Wells, Assistant Legal Adviser, Lloyds Bank Trust Division.)*

# The administration of legacy income

The proper administration of a Will depends on two factors; the first is a properly drawn up Will which contains explicit instructions as to how the estate should be distributed, and the second is the efficient and honest discharge of their duties by the Executors of the estate. Wherever possible people should have their Wills drawn up professionally. Home-made Wills can cause a lot of trouble, and in the end they may even fail to provide for the testator's instructions where they are drawn up defectively.

The administration of an estate is usually well under way before a charity gets involved. The first that the charity will normally hear about a Will in which it is named as a beneficiary is through the Smee and Ford notification service (if it subscribes to this). This service is described in detail in Appendix 4. Basically, for a small sum (currently £1.25 per notification) a charity is notified of its interest in a Will and of the names of the Executors as soon as the Will is probated. This is a very valuable service, as it gives the charity advance information of the legacies it will receive. It is best to leave a period of around six months between when the charity first hears of its interest in a Will through the Smee and Ford notification and contacting the Executors, as this will give the Executors a chance to sort things out and the time to contact the charity themselves.

On occasion a Will does not specifically mention a charity but leaves the Executors with the power to apply certain funds to charitable purposes in general, or to benefit particular types of charity. Smee and Ford provide a second service whereby they notify subscribing charities of situations where the charity might be eligible to receive a legacy under the terms of the Will, but where it is not specifically named as a beneficiary. When a charity receives this sort of notification, it will normally wish to make an application to the Executors; and it would probably wish to do this straight away rather than wait for several months.

Straight pecuniary sums are the simplest to administer from the beneficiary's point of view. This usually involves little more than a brief exchange of letters to establish the charity's right to the legacy and to have the money paid over. Most legacies received by charities are straight pecuniary sums. But there are two reasons why a charity might prefer to receive legacies in other forms. Firstly the value of a pecuniary legacy will decline with inflation, and at the time of the testator's death it may represent only a small fraction of the value of the gift that was intended in the first place. And secondly the testator himself might have received a legacy after he has drawn up his own Will, and this could affect his own financial circumstances very considerably; but unless he amended his Will, his pecuniary bequests would remain unaltered.

A bequest of a gift in kind (a house, items of furniture or jewellery, etc.) can also be simple to administer. When you are in receipt of such a gift and unless the gift is something intended for the charity's specific use, it should be your objective to convert the gift into cash at a realistic price. Charities can be bequeathed all manner of gifts:

'A reversion on an interest-free loan'

'All my National Savings Certificates'

'All my jewellery in my jewellery box'

'The contents of my account at . . . . . . . . . . bank'

'My fur coat'

'A plot of land'

'Everything in the dining room'

'All the contents of my house'

'The picture in the hall'

With this type of bequest the testator undoubtedly intended well, but it can on occasion cause problems. Firstly the assets bequeathed by the testator may not be there at the time of death. He may have sold his National Savings Certificates, the picture in the hall may no longer be there and his bank account may be in overdraft at the time of death. In these circumstances the intended beneficiary would not benefit. Secondly, it may be difficult to identify the asset – which picture in the hall as there may be two, one acquired subsequently to the Will having been made.

# THE ADMINISTRATION OF LEGACY INCOME

Although charities seldom get the opportunity of determining the nature of their bequests, the best type of legacy from the charity's point of view is the residue of the estate, or a share of it. The biggest single asset in most estates is a house. And the value of estates tends to rise and fall in line with property prices. Generally in the past property prices have tended to keep pace with inflation (or do better). Property is one of the few assets that has had sufficient capital growth to implement reliably the intentions of the testator during periods of high inflation. A residuary bequest will normally reflect any changes in the testator's means and protect its value in line with inflation.

Next let us look at some of the problem areas encountered in the administration of Wills where the charity is named as a residuary beneficiary:

## 1. Payments out of the residue

Where a charity is a residuary beneficiary, one problem is what expenses can be met from the funds of the estate. Certain charges must be met – funeral charges, legal charges for the administration of the estate, any debts of the estate, and payment of any Capital Transfer Tax that is due. Other expenses that are incurred will normally be acceptable as most solicitors do understand what a charity can and cannot do.

Any expenditure in the estate not authorised in the Will can only be embarked on with the consent of the residuary beneficiaries. Where a charity is a residuary beneficiary this expenditure will have to be met wholly or partly from funds which belong to the charity. Where funds are held under charitable trusts there is an obligation that they be applied to these charitable purposes. A charity has to be extremely careful in considering requests for unauthorised expenditure, and Executors must consult with the charity before actually incurring such expenditure. Charities should have due regard to the Charity Commissioners' guidelines on the subject of ex gratia payments from estates which are printed in Appendix 3.

In all dealings with the Executors and the family you should try to demonstrate competence and fairness. Try to respect the feelings of the bereaved first and foremost, and maintain a proper sense of dignity in whatever is done. Litigation can be bad PR, and a further legacy may be received from the same family at a later date if you have played fair with them.

## 2. Taxation

Relief from Capital Transfer Tax can be claimed if part or all of an estate passes to charity – and, broadly speaking, the benefits stemming from this should properly go to the charity beneficiaries. Any residuary beneficiary is entitled to receive the accounts of the estate. These should be sufficiently detailed to show the benefits of Capital Transfer Tax exemption, and that the charity beneficiaries have been granted their full entitlement. Where this has not been done properly, the charity should query the accounts before signing them. It may be that the benefit of the relief has inadvertently not been apportioned to the charity but been given to both the charitable and non-charitable beneficiaries, or it may not have been claimed in the first place. The charity should also check what Income Tax has been paid on any income earned by the estate whilst it is in the hands of the Executors. It will be entitled to reclaim its share of Income Tax suffered on income arising during administration of the estate. The charity should check that the income is either paid over gross without deduction of Income Tax, or if it is paid over net, then that a Certificate of Deduction of Tax is supplied by the Executors. This can then be submitted to the Inland Revenue Claims Branch and any Income Tax suffered can then be reclaimed. Some Executors use a Building Society account and under recent changes in procedure any Income Tax paid in respect of Building Society interest can now be reclaimed.

Although all assets passing on death are free from Capital Gains Tax, there may be changes in prevailing prices between probate and any subsequent sale, and the Executors may become liable to Capital Gains Tax when certain assets are realised by the estate. A charity beneficiary is exempt from Capital Gains Tax and no tax liability will be incurred if the disposal of the assets is handled properly. All securities have to be apportioned by the Executors to the residuary beneficiaries and this apportionment has to be clearly shown in the accounts. Any securities sold for cash are then sold on behalf of the residuary beneficiaries on a *'Bare Trustee'* basis. By adopting this procedure any Capital Gains Tax liability for the charity beneficiaries is avoided.

Every charity will experience cases from time to time where they have had to suffer Capital Gains Tax simply because the estate has not been administered properly. This is rare but it does happen.

An important distinction should be made between the sale of an asset by an Executor to raise funds to meet debts, funeral expenses, Capital Transfer Tax liability, pecuniary legacies and any administrative expenses, and the sale of an asset for the benefit of, or on behalf of, the residuary legatee(s). The *'Bare Trustee'* arrangements described above can only be applied in the second case, the former being *'Executor Sales'* and subject to Capital Gains Tax as may be.

### 3. Legal charges

All legal charges and administration expenses are met from the funds of the estate. Occasionally you may feel that the administration charge is too high and wish to raise the matter with the Executors. Either the charges will then be reduced or a good reason will emerge why they were high in the first place. There are two problems in trying to assess whether charges are fair or not. The first is that there is no standard scale of charging, and secondly the work involved may vary quite considerably depending on the nature of the estate.

Scale rates for the administration of Wills for the legal profession were abolished in 1972. The basis on which solicitors can charge is set out in the *1972 Solicitors Remuneration Order* and is based on the amount of work involved. It is not simply a matter of seeing what percentage of the gross value of the estate is charged, as a large estate may have been particularly simple to administer or a small estate extremely complicated. In the end you will have to use your own judgement as to whether the charges that are made are reasonable. Where the trust company of a bank is administering the Will, the charges that are levied will be according to a published scale of fees available from the bank concerned.

If you are not satisfied there are a number of things you can do:

(a) Ask your own solicitor for an opinion. He can then do whatever is necessary. If there are several residuary beneficiaries this can be done on a cost-sharing basis.

(b) Ask the Executors to refer the matter to the Law Society who can assess the reasonable cost and issue a Remuneration Certificate. Only the Executors can ask for a Remuneration Certificate, although the costs of administration are borne by the residuary beneficiaries. Where the Executors are the same people as the lawyers administering the estate, they may be unwilling to seek arbitration on costs. In these circumstances the charity beneficiary can approach the Law Society direct who will then use their influence to try to persuade the Executors to leave the matter arbitrated.

(c) Take the matter to the High Court for an 'Application for Taxation' under *Section 71* of the *1974 Solicitors Act*. This process involves three stages: first a summons is issued against the Solicitor, next there is a preliminary hearing where a decision is made on whether the application should be proceeded with and then there is a second hearing where the matter will be examined.

## 4. Period of administration

Normally a Will will be administered with reasonable efficiency. There are several things you can do when an administration appears to be unduly protracted:

(a) **Ask questions.** If you don't get answers, this should immediately produce warning signals. Make sure that you are satisfied with the answers, that they represent an accurate assessment of what is proving to be a difficult case, and that you are not being fobbed off. If you are receiving no replies at all to your enquiries or if you feel that the replies you are receiving are unsatisfactory, then contact the senior partner, state your anxiety, and ask him to deal with the problem. Use the telephone; it is more direct, and it may generate action more easily.

(b) **Co-operate** as much as possible with the other residuary beneficiaries. The administration cannot be wound up until there is agreement between all the residuary beneficiaries over any problems that have arisen. Where you are sole beneficiary, what you do is your decision alone. Where there are others try to liaise with everybody. Try to get an agreed line of approach, as this will help you deal with the Executors. Again use the telephone; it may then take minutes to resolve what might otherwise take months. Where the beneficiaries consist of charities and adult individuals, then if there are problems a meeting can be arranged to sort out any outstanding difficulties. Where infant or as yet unborn beneficiaries are involved then matters may be more difficult. The Trustees may be able to use their discretion, but the matter may need to go to Court for resolution.

The larger charities are often in touch with each other over Wills where they are co-beneficiaries. So their legacy officers know one another and are used to dealing with each other. Smaller charities have the opportunity to collaborate too, and should be encouraged to do so. But co-operation and finding an agreed position should not blur the fact that a charity may need to protect its own special interests. There may be a conflict of interest between the charities concerned with regard to a particular Will. Different charities operate in very different fields; and the differing interests need to be respected and taken into account. It will usually be possible to negotiate a reasonable compromise, acceptable to all concerned; and if practicable, it is extremely beneficial for the charities to work together to get the maximum benefit for all who are to benefit from the Will.

(c) **Go to law** if necessary, but remember that litigation is expensive and should not be entered into without your being fully aware of the costs involved. On occasion litigation may be the only way of resolving an issue, and if it is appropriate to proceed on a cost-sharing basis with other beneficiaries, then this should be explored.

Finally, in your dealings with solicitors try to be efficient and courteous. There is a public relations aspect to all your correspondence and other dealings with Executor Banks and Solicitors which should not be underestimated.

# APPENDICES

Taxation and legacy income
Provisions for family and dependants
Ex-gratia payments by charities
Smee and Ford notification service
Resources

# APPENDIX 1

# Taxation and Legacy Income

A legacy bequeathed to a charity (or any other charitable gifts made on death) is neutral for tax purposes. There is no actual tax benefit to the recipient charity, as there is with lifetime donations made under Deed of Covenant for example. On the other hand Capital Transfer Tax may be payable on gifts which are not made to charity. The tax benefit only exists in relation to the tax that would be payable if the donor gave the same gift to another person (or to a non-charitable organisation) and incurred a tax liability in the process of so doing.

To understand fully the tax benefits of giving to charity on death, you need to understand the working of Capital Transfer Tax (CTT) and Capital Gains Tax (CGT), when these taxes are chargeable and what transfers are exempted. And you also need to understand the tax situation for giving to charity by making a lifetime gift of capital and by making a gift out of income under Deed of Covenant.

Capital Transfer Tax and Capital Gains Tax are extremely complicated taxes and many of their ramifications are beyond the scope of this book. Tax planning to reduce an individual's liability to capital taxes during his lifetime and on death is also a complicated subject. What we have tried to do in this section is to give a general picture of how these two taxes work in relation to capital gifts, of what gifts are exempt and when these taxes are chargeable. We also examine the tax situation in relation to lifetime gifts made out of the donor's income under a Deed of Covenant. This will show the relative benefits of making a lifetime gift out of income or capital and of giving on death through a legacy or bequest. Armed with the facts and figures, charities should be able to understand the tax advantages of receiving money in various ways; and this should help them plan their fund-raising strategy and determine the best approach for encouraging their supporters (and the general public) to give.

**Note:** The tax rates and thresholds stated in this section are those that are applicable for 1983–84. References to the *1983 Finance Act* include the *1983 Finance Act* taken together with the *1983 Finance (No. 2) Act*. At the time of writing the provisions of the *1983 Finance (No. 2) Act* had not been formally enacted, and any changes that may have been made to the Finance Bill in its passage through Parliament will not have been included.

# 1. Gifts made on death

## How Capital Transfer Tax works

Capital Transfer Tax is charged on the adjusted gross value (*see below*) of the assets of a deceased person passing on death, whether under the terms of a Will or, where there is no valid Will, under the Intestacy Rules. It is payable on all the property of people domiciled in the UK, and on the UK property only of people domiciled elsewhere. Capital Transfer Tax was introduced from 27 March 1974 and is levied on the estates of people dying on or after that date (it is also levied on lifetime transfers made on or after that date, for which different rates of tax apply). Capital Transfer Tax replaced the old Estate Duty levy.

Capital Transfer Tax is payable on 'chargeable transfers' of assets passing on death. Not all transfers are chargeable. What is chargeable and what is not depends on whom the assets are bequeathed to. In particular, assets passing to the spouse of the deceased and assets bequeathed to charity are exempt and are not included when calculating the level of chargeable transfers. Tax is chargeable on a sliding scale starting at a nil rate and rising up to a maximum rate of 75%.

Capital Transfer Tax is a cumulative tax levied on assets transferred during your lifetime and on your death. The rate of tax that is chargeable on your estate will depend not only on the value of your estate, but it will also be affected by the total amount of chargeable transfers you have made in the 10-year period up to your death.

All assets are assessed for tax at their current value (which is their probate value). No Capital Gains Tax is payable in respect of transfers on death, even where the probate value is in excess of the original purchase price of the asset. The deemed purchase price for the beneficiary receiving an asset from the deceased's estate for his own Capital Gains Tax purposes is the probate value at which the asset was transferred, and not its original purchase price.

The rates of Capital Transfer Tax are:

| Amount of chargeable transfers* | Rate of Tax | Cumulative value of chargeable transfers* | Cumulative Capital Transfer Tax payable |
|---|---|---|---|
| **The first** | | | |
| £60,000 | NIL | 60,000 | NIL |
| **The next** | | | |
| £20,000 | 30% | 80,000 | 6,000 |
| £30,000 | 35% | 110,000 | 16,500 |
| £30,000 | 40% | 140,000 | 28,500 |
| £35,000 | 45% | 175,000 | 44,250 |
| £45,000 | 50% | 220,000 | 66,750 |
| £50,000 | 55% | 270,000 | 94,250 |
| £430,000 | 60% | 700,000 | 352,250 |
| £625,000 | 65% | 1,325,000 | 758,500 |
| £1,325,000 | 70% | 2,650,000 | 1,686,000 |
| **The remainder of the estate** | 75% | over 2,650,000 | |

\* *Note: in calculating the amount of tax that is payable, all chargeable transfers made by the deceased in the 10-year period up to his death are taken into account, and these are added to the chargeable transfers passing on death.*

These rates for the 1983–84 financial year and apply for all transfers on or after 15th March 1983. Under the *1982 Finance Act* the bands at which the different rates are chargeable became linked to the Retail Prices Index and will be adjusted each year unless and until Parliament decides otherwise. This statutory method of adjusting the Capital Transfer Tax bands is detailed in the *1982 Finance Act*, and works as follows:

The statutory method of indexation of tax bands for any tax year is based on the annual rate of increase in the Retail Prices Index during the 12-month period up to and including the previous December. This rate of inflation is then used to increase the tax bands that applied for the previous year, which are then rounded up to a multiple of £1,000. Should there be any decline in the Retail Prices Index, the rates for the previous year will continue. Thus the tax bands will be raised at a rate slightly higher than the rate of inflation because of the rounding up process (which is the benefit of those who have to pay the tax generally).

It is simplest to show how this indexation works through an example. For 1982–83 the nil tax band applied to chargeable transfers up to £55,000. The inflation rate for the year to December 1982 was 5.4%. For 1983–84 under the statutory indexation procedure, the nil tax band was increased from £55,000 to £57,970 and then rounded up to £58,000 for 1983–84. However, in the 1983 Budget the Government decided to increase the tax thresholds for Capital Transfer Tax beyond what was required under the statutory indexation procedure, and the nil tax band for 1983–84 was set at £60,000. Similarly, higher than inflation increases were applied to the other tax bands. For 1984–85 under the index-linking procedure, the nil tax band will be calculated by increasing its present £60,000 level by the annual inflation in the Retail Prices Index for the 12-month period ending December 1983, and again rounding up to the nearest £1,000. The other bands will be increased similarly; and the new bands will apply from 6th April 1984. And this process will continue from year to year until the system is changed.

## What assets are chargeable

In calculating the amount of Capital Transfer Tax that is payable, several adjustments have to be made to the gross value of the estate:

1. **Certain deductions are made from the gross value of the assets of the deceased person**

   (a) Any non-qualifying (excluded) property (which applies largely to people domiciled overseas).

   (b) Any UK debts owed at the date of death and any liability to Income Tax and Capital Gains Tax in respect of the period up to death, even where no assessment has been made prior to death.

   (c) Funeral expenses, but not other legal and professional fees.

The general rule on expenses is that any expenses incurred after the death of the testator are not deductible when calculating the Capital Transfer Tax liability of the estate. Thus any legal or professional fees incurred on the administration of the estate after death are not deductible. The cost of reasonable funeral expenses is deductible, and in calculating the amount of these expenses no account need be taken of any death grant received. The cost of providing a tombstone is specifically excluded and is not deductible. Where an estate contains property situated outside the UK certain expenses may be deducted which are incurred in the administration or disposal of such property. These expenses are limited to the total actually incurred up to a maximum of 5% of the value of the property.

This adjusted value of the deceased's assets is known as the net value of the estate, and this net value is the basis on which any liability to Capital Transfer is calculated.

## 2. Certain 'exempt transfers' are then deducted from the net value of the estate chargeable to Capital Transfer Tax

The main exemption is for all property passing to a surviving husband or wife. Other exemptions that are of interest to charities are:

(a) Charitable gifts of any amount. Note that up until 1983 there was a limit of £250,000 on the amount that could be given to charity by any person in the last year of his life and on his death which was exempt from Capital Transfer Tax). A charity only falls within this exemption if it is established within the UK. A charitable gift is a gift given to a charity for its charitable purposes or held in trust for charitable purposes only.

(b) Gifts to national institutions (as specified in *Schedule 6(12)* of the *1975 Finance Act*. The institutions for which the exemption applies are:

The National Gallery
The British Museum
The Royal Scottish Museum
The National Museum of Wales
The Ulster Museum

Any other similar national institution which exists wholly or mainly for the purpose of preserving for the public benefit a collection of scientific, historic or artistic interest and which is approved for this purpose by the Treasury. The following institutions fall within this category: British Museum (National History); Science Museum; Victoria and Albert Museum; Imperial War Museum; Museum of London; National Maritime Museum; National Portrait Gallery; Tate Gallery; Wallace Collection; Geological Museum; National Galleries of Scotland; National Museum of Antiquities of Scotland; National Library of Scotland; National Library of Wales; Ulster Folk Museum; The British Library; National Army Museum; Royal Marine Museum; Submarine Museum; Tower Armouries; RAF Museum; Fleet Air Arm Museum.

Any museum or art gallery maintained by a university or local authority in the UK

Any library whose main function is to serve the needs of teaching and research at a university in the UK.

The National Trust and the Scottish National Trust.

The National Art Collections Fund

The Friends of the National Libraries

The Historic Churches Preservation Trust

The Nature Conservancy Council

Any local authority

The National Debt Commissioners and any government department

Any university or university college in the UK

Gifts of unlimited amount to these institutions are exempt. Up until the *1983 Finance Act* there was a limit of £250,000 on the exemption of gifts to charities and gifts could be made over and above this limit to the national institutions listed here. Now that this limit has been dropped many of the bodies listed here would also be exempt by virtue of their charitable status.

(c) Gifts to political parties of up to £100,000, and in this total are included any gifts made in the 12 months prior to death. A 'political party' is defined for the purposes of this exemption as requiring:

1. At least two sitting MPs elected as members of that party at the last general election, or

2. One sitting MP and having obtained not less than 150,000 votes for its candidates at the last General Election.

(d) Gifts for public benefit: Gifts of unlimited amount of certain property which are deemed by the Treasury to be of outstanding scenic, historic, artistic or scientific merit when given to a body which is neither established nor conducted for profit are exempt. Recipients might include local preservation groups and amenity societies. This exemption will now have only limited application as most non-profit bodies will be established as charities and will therefore be entitled to exemption on that basis. Where this exemption applies the Treasury will make its decision based on the nature of the property bequeathed as well as the suitability of the recipient as custodian of the property. Property falling within this exemption includes:

Land

Buildings with surrounding land used as its grounds and objects given with the building which are ordinarily kept in it

Pictures, prints, books, manuscripts, works of art, scientific objects.

In addition any property or endowment provided for the upkeep of the above property also falls within this exemption. Before granting the exemption the Treasury can require undertakings to be entered into (for example restricting use or disposal or conditions of public access). The Treasury may also accept such items in lieu of payment of Capital Transfer Tax.

These exemptions are granted subject to certain conditions; the main conditions are:

1. The property should pass immediately to the beneficiary. The exemption does not apply for reversionary gifts – for example, if a life interest in the property is given to the surviving spouse or if the property is to be held for the benefit of a son or daughter until the age of 21 and the gift passes to the charity at the end of the specified period. But the transfer of the property to the charity at the end of any intermediate interest is exempt.

2. The gift is unconditional, or if there is a condition attached to the gift then that condition must be satisfied within a

12-month period of the gift being made. If the condition is capable of being satisfied within the stated period, then Capital Transfer Tax will not be chargeable immediately, but it will become chargeable if the condition is not met.

3. The gift is not capable of cancellation (defeasible), and it is treated as not being defeasible if it has not been cancelled within 12 months of the gift being made and is not defeasible thereafter.

4. The gift must be given absolutely. It will not fall within the exemption if it is given for a limited period only.

5. The gift must represent the whole interest of the donor in the property at the time when the gift is made. For example where the freehold is owned, the exemption will not apply if the recipient body receives the property subject to a lease in favour of someone else, or if it receives only a leasehold interest in the property. Where only a leasehold or reversionary interest in the property is owned by the donor then that interest can be transferred within the exemption. If the deceased creates an interest which terminates within 12 months of the gift then the exemption will still apply.

6. There is no reservation of benefit by the donor – for example any building or land given subject to an entitlement that his spouse or a person connected with him or his successors occupy all or a part of the property rent free or at a rent less than that which might be expected in an arms-length transaction is not exempt.

7. The gift is not capable of application for purposes other than those of the recipient body to which it was given. However, subject to no binding trust to the contrary, the recipient body is permitted to sell the gift and apply the proceeds of the sale for its own purposes.

Most charitable legacies consist of sums of money or other property given absolutely. Where the testator wishes to bequeath a legacy subject to certain conditions or subject to certain interests being reserved then he is advised to take proper legal advice.

3. **The amount of any chargeable capital transfers made in the 10 years preceding death (but excluding any transfers made before 27th March 1974) is taken into account when calculating the rates of Capital Transfer Tax that are chargeable**

The amount given away in the 10-year period is offset against the £60,000 exemption limit; and if more than £60,000 is given away, any excess beyond this amount is progressively offset against the lowest tax bands. The effect of this is to push the estate passing on death into higher and higher tax bands as the following example shows:

The table below shows how the Capital Transfer Tax payable on a £100,000 estate is affected by chargeable transfers made in the 10-year period prior to death:

| Tax band: | Amount of estate chargeable: | | | |
|---|---|---|---|---|
| Value of transfers made in 10 years prior to death | NIL | £25,000 | £50,000 | £75,000 |
| NIL | 60,000 | 35,000 | 10,000 | — |
| 30% | 20,000 | 20,000 | 20,000 | 5,000 |
| 35% | 20,000 | 30,000 | 30,000 | 30,000 |
| 40% | — | 15,000 | 30,000 | 30,000 |
| 45% | — | — | 10,000 | 35,000 |
| 50% | — | — | — | — |
| 55% | — | — | — | — |
| 60% | — | — | — | — |
| 65% | — | — | — | — |
| 70% | — | — | — | — |
| 75% | — | — | — | — |
| **Total tax payable** | 13,000 | 22,500 | 33,000 | 40,250 |

4. **Any amounts which have been given away in the three years prior to death and on which Capital Transfer Tax has already been levied at the lifetime rates will become liable to Capital Transfer Tax at the rates for transfers passing on death**

The lifetime rates of Capital Transfer Tax are lower than the 'on death' rates, and the additional tax payable will be assessed on the difference between the on-death rate at the time of death and the lifetime rate at which the tax was actually paid.

## Who pays Capital Transfer Tax

Capital Transfer Tax payable on an estate passing on death will be paid out of the property comprised in the estate. The normal rule is that:

1. Where the testator directs how the tax should be paid, for example by stating that certain bequests are free of tax, then the Executors will be bound by this direction (subject to there being sufficient funds in the estate).

2. Where no specific direction is given, then Capital Transfer Tax is a testamentary expense and is payable from the residue of the estate – thereby reducing the amount available for the residuary beneficiaries.

3. Where there are insufficient funds in the residue of the estate to meet the Capital Transfer Tax liability, then the tax that is payable in excess of the residue of the estate will be apportioned amongst the beneficiaries.

4. Where a beneficiary is exempt (surviving spouse, charity, political party, gift for national purposes or for public benefit), this will reduce the amount of tax that is payable. Where a charity beneficiary receives a specific bequest then it will receive the whole of that bequest regardless of whether there are sufficient funds in the residue to meet the Capital Transfer Tax liability. Where a charity beneficiary is entitled to the residue (or a share of the residue) of the estate, the tax will be paid out of its share of the estate reducing the amount available for distribution, although it will enjoy the benefit of its exemption in respect of the amount it actually receives.

There has been a recent change in the law concerning the treatment of real estate or realty (which is land and property) as distinct from personalty (which is all other assets including cash, stocks and shares, personal chattels, etc.). In the *1983 Finance Act*, Capital Transfer Tax on real estate was deemed to be a testamentary expense, and became payable out of the residue of the estate in the absence of any contrary intention by the testator.

Up until 1981 any Capital Transfer Tax payable in respect of a gift of realty was paid by the beneficiary of that gift. This was the position for Estate Duty prior to the introduction of Capital Transfer Tax, and it was the intention that the situation should remain the same for Capital Transfer Tax. However in the Scottish Courts in re Dougal the Court decided that the 1975 Finance Act, which introduced Capital Transfer Tax, had made a radical change in the law, and that no distinction should now be made between realty and personalty. As a result of this decision, in Scotland Capital Transfer Tax was deemed to be a testamentary expense for gifts of realty.

Although English Courts were not bound by decisions in the Scottish Courts and no similar case reached the English Courts, the Inland Revenue advised that there was no essential difference between Scottish Law and English law with regard to Capital Transfer Tax. This left a confused situation which meant that the specific and residuary beneficiaries had to agree on who should bear the Capital Transfer Tax due on a gift of realty, or where the beneficiaries could not reach agreement, then the Inland Revenue would follow the decision of re Dougal until and unless the English Courts decided otherwise or the matter was clarified by amending legislation. This clarification was introduced in the 1983 Finance Act. The beneficiary of a gift of real estate is no longer liable to pay Capital Transfer Tax in respect of that gift, subject to there being sufficient funds in the residue of the estate to meet the Capital Transfer Tax liability. Any mortgage or other charge on the assets, however, passes to the recipient along with the asset (unless stated to the contrary in the Will).

Although a charity beneficiary is an exempt beneficiary, it will be affected by Capital Transfer Tax in a number of ways:

1. Where the charity is a residuary legatee all testamentary expenses, including Capital Transfer Tax will be a charge on the residue of the estate and reduce the amount available for the residuary beneficiaries.

2. Because of its exempt status, no Capital Transfer Tax will be payable in respect of the legacy received by the charity. The charity must ensure that it receives full benefit from this exemption and that the saving in Capital Transfer Tax is not apportioned equally amongst all the beneficiaries.

3. Because of its exempt status there will be a saving in Capital Transfer Tax liability where the legacy would otherwise

have gone to a non-exempt beneficiary. This should be a 'selling point' when charities try to persuade their supporters to leave them a legacy. The saving will be as follows for a legacy of £1,000:

| Top rate of tax on the estate | Tax saving | Cost of the £1,000 legacy to the estate | Tax advantage |
|---|---|---|---|
| 30% | £300 | £700 | +43% |
| 35% | £350 | £650 | +54% |
| 40% | £400 | £600 | +67% |
| 45% | £450 | £550 | +82% |
| 50% | £500 | £500 | +100% |
| 55% | £550 | £450 | +122% |
| 60% | £600 | £400 | +150% |
| 65% | £650 | £350 | +186% |
| 70% | £700 | £300 | +233% |
| 75% | £750 | £250 | +300% |

# 2. Lifetime Capital Gifts

## Capital Transfer Tax on gifts to charity

A lifetime gift of any size made to a charity (or for charitable purposes) is free from Capital Transfer Tax provided that the charity is established in the UK and the gift is applied for charitable purposes. Certain other conditions have to be met; these conditions are the same as for gifts passing to charity on death (see page 119).

In addition, if the gift is a gift in kind then it is also free of any Capital Gains Tax. A transfer of an asset to a charity is treated for tax purposes as a disposal on which neither a gain nor a loss is made regardless of the original purchase price of the asset.

Thus lifetime gifts to charity are exempt from tax in almost all circumstances. The following are examples of gifts which would not be covered by the exemption:

1. Gifts to non-UK charities.
2. Gifts to a benevolent or voluntary organisation which is not a charity; but where there is a condition attached to the gift that it is to be applied for charitable purposes only, then the exemption will normally apply.

3. A life interest or a reversionary interest in the asset. For the exemption to apply the asset must be given absolutely.

4. Where the gift is conditional and the condition is not met within one year. The most common situation is where a gift is made for the second stage of a building programme conditional on the first stage being completed, or for an appeal conditional on the organisation itself raising a specified amount in addition to the gift.

## Capital Transfer Tax on other gifts

Where the beneficiary is not a charity then a gift may be subject to Capital Transfer Tax. Certain transfers are completely exempt from Capital Transfer Tax:

1. All gifts from a husband to wife or from a wife to a husband.

2. Gifts for the maintenance, care or education of your ex-wife, your child (including illegitimate child and a child not in his parents' care who has been in your care during a substantial period of his childhood), or any dependent relatives.

3. Gifts in consideration of marriage to either marriage partner by any parent of one of the marriage partners of up to £5,000 or by any grandparent of up to £2,500 or by any other person of up to £1,000.

4. Gifts to political parties of unlimited amount (although there is a limit if the gift is made in the last year of the donor's life) and gifts for national purposes and gifts of property deemed by the Treasury to be for public benefit of unlimited amount.

5. Gifts made out of income to the extent that such gifts represent normal expenditure out of the donor's income. Capital Transfer Tax only applies to capital gifts.

There are also concessions in respect of certain small gifts which are exempt from Capital Transfer Tax regardless of the beneficiary:

(a) Any gift of up to a total of £250 to any beneficiary in any year.

(b) For gifts exceeding £250 per beneficiary, a total of £3,000 may be given away in any year. If the whole of this £3,000 exemption limit is not used, any unused balance may be carried forward to the next year only. In calculating the used balance for any year, gifts in that year are set against the exemption for that year in priority to being set against any unused balance brought forward from the previous year. The year that applies is the tax year from 6th April to the subsequent 5th April.

These exemptions are available for gifts made by a husband and for gifts made by a wife. Any gifts in excess of these amounts will be chargeable to Capital Transfer Tax. However, transfers up to a certain level can be made without incurring any liability to Capital Transfer Tax, since the first tranche of chargeable transfers are assessed to tax at a nil rate band. The Capital Transfer Tax rates on lifetime transfers are as follows (1983–84 figures):

| Amount of chargeable transfers* | Rate of Tax | Cumulative value of lifetime transfers** |
|---|---|---|
| **The first** | | |
| £60,000 | NIL | £60,000 |
| **The next** | | |
| £20,000 | 15% | £80,000 |
| £30,000 | 17½% | £110,000 |
| £30,000 | 20% | £140,000 |
| £35,000 | 22½% | £175,000 |
| £45,000 | 25% | £220,000 |
| £50,000 | 30% | £270,000 |
| £430,000 | 35% | £700,000 |
| £625,000 | 40% | £1,325,000 |
| £1,325,000 | 45% | £2,650,000 |
| **The remainder over and above this amount** | 50% | over £2.65 million |

\* These rate bands are for 1983–84 and, unless and until Parliament decides otherwise, are changed annually in order to take inflation into account (see below).

\*\* Cumulative total refers to all transfers made in the 10-year period up to and including the year in which the gift is being made (see below).

126

Capital Transfer Tax is a cumulative tax levied on the value of all chargeable transfers made in any 10-year period. The amount of tax payable on a transfer depends on the value of that transfer and on the total transfers made by that individual during the previous 10 years. The more that has been transferred during that 10-year period, the higher will be the rate of tax levied on the transfer being made. Capital Transfer Tax was introduced from 26th March 1974 and only transfers made subsequent to that date are chargeable. The 10-year limit on cumulation was introduced in the *1981 Finance Act*; previously all chargeable transfers made during an individual's lifetime had to be taken into account. Where a asset is sold at less than its market value, the difference between the sale price and the value of the asset is treated as a gift for Capital Transfer Tax purposes.

The thresholds for the various tax bands are indexed with the rate of inflation. The basis on which they are altered each year is exactly the same as for on-death transfers, where the tax bands are identical although the rates of tax that are chargeable are higher (*see page 115*). Where a person dies within three years of making a chargeable transfer on which tax has been paid at the lifetime rate, then there is an additional liability to tax calculated on the difference between the lifetime rate and the on-death rate.

Because of the 'rounding up' procedure the tax bands will be increased at a rate slightly greater than the rate of inflation (which is to the benefit of the taxpayer). And because only the tax bands and not the amounts that have been given away in previous years are indexed in making the calculation of Capital Transfer Tax liability on chargeable transfers, it in fact pays an individual to give money away within the nil tax band sooner rather than later, as this will increase the real value of the cumulative gifts that can be made within the nil tax band.

Thus an individual who has not yet made any chargeable transfers can give away £60,000 in 1983–84 in addition to any exemptions to which he is entitled without incurring any liability to Capital Transfer Tax. He will also be able to give away further sums over the next 10 years without incurring any liability to Capital Transfer Tax. This will top up the total of all chargeable transfers made in order to allow for the effect of inflation on the nil tax band. And after 10 years from the date of the original gift, the amount of that gift (£60,000 in this example) will be dropped from the calculations, and further transfers up to the limit of the nil rate band can then be made.

Capital Transfer Tax can be paid either by the donor or by the recipient. Who pays will depend on the terms on which the gift was made. If it is paid by the recipient of the gift, the rate at which it will be charged is the value of the gift multiplied by the appropriate tax rate(s) for the tax band(s) within which the gift falls. If it is paid by the donor the value of the gift has to be 'grossed up' for tax purposes such that the net amount after deduction of the Capital Transfer Tax that is payable is equal to the value of the gift. Thus more Capital Transfer Tax will be payable if the donor pays the tax, but the recipient will not be liable to tax.

The effect of this grossing up can be illustrated by an example. If a person makes a chargeable transfer of £10,000, all of which falls in the 15% rate band, then if Capital Transfer Tax is payable by the recipient the amount of tax that is payable will equal £1,500. If the tax is paid by the donor, in order that the recipient receives £10,000 after tax, the donor would have to make a gift of £11,765, since tax at 15% on this amount equals £1,765.

The lifetime rates for Capital Transfer Tax are substantially lower than the 'on death' rates. For cash gifts any tax liability will be reduced by making the transfers during the person's lifetime rather than on death.

## Liability of gifts to Capital Gains Tax

For gifts in kind the donor may be liable to Capital Gains Tax in addition to Capital Transfer Tax. For cash gifts there will, of course, be no liability at all to Capital Gains Tax. The basis of assessment to Capital Gains Tax is completely independent of the basis of assessment to Capital Transfer Tax. Thus a gift may be liable to Capital Transfer Tax but not to Capital Gains Tax, or it may be liable to Capital Gains Tax but not to Capital Transfer Tax, or it may be liable to both or to neither.

An asset does not have to be sold in order to incur a Capital Gains Tax liability. A gift is treated as a disposition for Capital Gains Tax purposes, and the price at which the disposition was made is deemed to be the value of the gift at the date on which the transfer was made. And the same is true for the sale of an asset at less than its market value. Certain gifts are exempt. The main exemptions are:

1. All gifts to charities are exempt from Capital Gains Tax (under *Section 145* of the *1979 Capital Gains Tax Act* such a disposition is treated as a disposal on which neither a loss nor a gain is made). So gifts to charity (including sales at below market value) are completely tax free.

2. All gifts made from a husband to a wife or vice versa provided they are living together, are exempt from Capital Gains Tax, but the assumed purchase price of the asset for Capital Gains Tax purposes when the recipient sells it is its original purchase price, not the value at the date the transfer was made.

3. All gifts of wasting assets which are also movable property (chattels) are normally exempt from Capital Gains Tax. A wasting asset is defined as an asset with a predictable life not exceeding 50 years. This covers such things as boats, aircraft, animals, etc.

4. All gifts of movable property with a value of less than £3,000 are exempt from Capital Gains Tax. For this purpose a set of objects is treated as one item (a pair of candlesticks, a set of six dining chairs, etc.). Where the gift is valued at over £3,000 the gain is limited to five thirds of the excess of the transfer value over £3,000 or the actual gain, whichever is the lesser. If the asset was purchased for more than £3,000 and is sold for less than £3,000 the extent of the loss that can be offset against any capital gain is restricted to the difference between the purchase price and £3,000. This exemption from Capital Gains Tax in respect of movable property covers any number of dispositions made during any year.

5. A gift of property deemed to be of national interest together with any funds settled for its upkeep is exempt from Capital Gains Tax provided there is public access.

6. A gift of your only or main private residence is exempt.

7. Small gifts totalling not more than £100 in value given to any individual in any tax year are exempt.

All other gifts are chargeable to Capital Gains Tax. There is an annual exemption of the first £5,300 of chargeable gains incurred by an individual (which includes any gains on assets disposed of by your wife/husband). In addition any losses brought forward from the previous year may be offset against any gains made during the year. The annual £5,300 exemption is used first to reduce any Capital Gains Tax liability before offsetting the losses brought forward. Any unused losses are carried forward from year to year until they are used up. But if any part of the £5,300 exemption limit is unused, it cannot be carried forward for use in the next year. The tax year runs from 6th April to the subsequent 5th April.

Since April 1982 allowance can be made for the effect of inflation in calculating the liability to Capital Gains Tax. Assets have to be held for at least one year, and indexation commences on 5th April 1982 for assets purchased prior to 5th April 1981 or exactly one year after the date of purchase for assets purchased subsequently. The purchase price of the asset is increased by the rate of inflation (as measured by the Retail Prices Index) from the date on which indexation starts until the date of sale. Thus for an asset purchased for £100 and sold exactly two years later, where the annual rate of inflation is constant at 10 per cent, the indexed purchase price for Capital Gains Tax is £110, and if the asset is sold at £200 the chargeable gain is £90. This indexation procedure cannot be used to create a capital loss.

The present rate of Capital Gains Tax (1983–84) is 30 per cent and is charged on any net capital gains after allowing for exempt dispositions, and for the annual exemption limit of £5,300 and for any losses brought forward. The rate of tax is constant; it does not increase progressively with the total amount of any gains made during any year.

So a donor making a chargeable transfer during his lifetime may at the same time also be making a chargeable gain. The fact that Capital Gains Tax is payable does not reduce the transfer price for Capital Transfer Tax purposes. The total tax payable (Capital Gains Tax and Capital Transfer Tax) can in some cases exceed the Capital Transfer Tax that would be payable if the gift were made on death. To take an extreme example:

For an asset purchased for 1 penny, which is transferred when it has a value of £1,000 – assuming the whole of the £5,300 annual exemption has been used up and assuming that the transfer falls within the £60,000–£80,000 rate band and that

Capital Transfer Tax is paid by the donor – the tax payable is as follows:

| | Lifetime | On Death |
|---|---|---|
| Capital Transfer Tax | £176 | £428 |
| Capital Gains Tax | £300 | – |
| **Total tax payable** | **£476** | **£428** |

But in most circumstances the total tax payable on lifetime gifts will be less than the Capital Transfer Tax payable on the same asset transferred on death.

# 3. Lifetime gifts out of income

## Covenanted donations

If a donor gives to charity out of his income under a Deed of Covenant, there are important tax advantages. The detailed mechanisms of covenanted giving are beyond the scope of this book. For further information the reader should see *'Covenants: a practical guide to the tax advantages of giving'*. But the essentials are that:

1. The donation should be paid out of the donor's income. A covenanted payment is not a capital gift and is not subject to Capital Transfer Tax. A donor should only make donations under Deed of Covenant on a scale which can reasonably be made out of his income, if he is to obtain the tax advantage.
2. The donor should be paying Income Tax at least at the basic rate, otherwise there can be complications.
3. The covenant should involve at least four annual payments. If it is not capable of lasting for at least four years, then it will not be effective for tax purposes.

If these three conditions are met, then the charity can reclaim Income Tax at the basic rate (30 per cent in 1982–83) in respect of the annual payment it has received under the covenant. For a £10 donation paid by a donor net out of his taxed income, the charity will be able to reclaim £4.28 from the Inland Revenue.

Since April 1981 the donor has also been able to set off his covenant payments to charity against his higher rate tax liability. This Higher Rate Relief is subject to a maximum of gross covenant payments of £5,000 per annum (and this is also the maximum for the combined covenant payments made by a husband and wife). The gross value of the covenant payment is the amount actually paid to the charity by the donor PLUS the Income Tax that the charity can reclaim. The maximum amount of net covenant payments that can be made in any year and on which Higher Rate Relief can be claimed is £3,500. Beyond this amount the charity will still be able to reclaim Income Tax at the basic rate, but no further Higher Rate Relief will be available to the donor.

The mechanics of Higher Rate Relief are quite complicated and are best illustrated by an example:

1. A donor pays tax at 50% and makes a £10 covenant payment to charity.
2. The charity will reclaim £4.28 in Income Tax in respect of the £10 'net' donation.
3. The 'gross' value of the covenant payment is £14.28.
4. The donor can offset £14.28 against his higher rate tax.
5. But relief is only given in respect of any tax paid by the donor in excess of the basic rate, since the charity has already benefited from tax relief at the basic rate.
6. The relief in this example is worth (50% − 30%) × £14.28 = £2.86.

With a 30% basic rate of Income Tax, the following are the benefits to the donor and charity of a £10 covenant payment:

| The donor pays Income Tax at | Higher Rate Relief on a £10 covenant payment | Cost to the donor | Value to the charity |
|---|---|---|---|
| 30% | NIL | £10.00 | £14.28 |
| 40% | £1.43 | £8.57 | £14.28 |
| 45% | £2.16 | £7.86 | £14.28 |
| 50% | £2.86 | £7.14 | £14.28 |
| 55% | £3.57 | £6.43 | £14.28 |
| 60% | £4.29 | £5.71 | £14.28 |
| 65% | £5.00 | £5.00 | £14.28 |
| 70% | £5.71 | £4.29 | £14.28 |
| 75% | £6.43 | £3.57 | £14.28 |

## Loan-covenants or deposited covenants

The main problem of a covenant is that it should consist of at least four annual payments. Many of a charity's supporters do not like to commit themselves to a particular charity over a number of years, and the charity itself will only receive the money in annual instalments and not all at once.

The advantages of giving under Deed of Covenant can be obtained for a single donation made by an individual to a charity using an ingenious device known as a 'Loan-Covenant' or a 'Deposited Covenant'.

The mechanism is that the donor lends the charity a certain sum interest-free, and at the same time enters into a Deed of Covenant in favour of the charity. The size of the loan will normally be four times the net annual payments due each year under the Deed of Covenant. And the repayment of the loan by the charity to the donor will be in four instalments, each instalment coinciding with the due date of the annual covenant payment. With this arrangement the loan repayment instalment and annual covenant payment exactly cancel each other out. No cash need actually change hands apart from the amount that is originally lent, but the charity can obtain the tax advantages on the four covenant payments as they fall due.

For annual covenant payments under £130 (net), there is a special scheme operated by the Inland Revenue whereby the donor only has to sign a Certificate of Deduction of Tax in the first year. For larger amounts a Certificate will have to be signed each year for the duration of the covenant.

The terms of the loan-covenant usually provide that in the event of the donor's death the covenant payments shall cease and the whole of the outstanding loan shall be converted into a gift. This avoids problems with the deceased's estate, although the charity will only be able to obtain tax benefit in respect of the covenant payments made before the death of the donor.

A loan-covenant may seem complicated, but it involves the donor in making one single payment for the amount he wishes to give (in the example on the next page £1,000), and in completing and signing various forms. For sums larger than £520 a Certificate of Deduction of Tax will have to be signed in subsequent years; but even this can be avoided if the donor splits the total into more than one Deed of Covenant and makes sure that no single Deed involves annual payments in excess of £130.

The workings of a Loan-Covenant can best be illustrated by an example:

**For a donor paying tax at 50%**

| On the due date in | Year 1 | Year 2 | Year 3 | Year 4 |
|---|---|---|---|---|
| **The donor pays** | | | | |
| Loan* | (1000) | | | |
| Covenant payment | (250) | (250) | (250) | (250) |
| **The donor receives**\** | | | | |
| Loan repayment | 250 | 250 | 250 | 250 |
| **Total payments** | (1000) | — | — | — |

**For a donor paying tax at 50%**

| On the due date in | Year 1 | Year 2 | Year 3 | Year 4 |
|---|---|---|---|---|
| **The charity receives** | | | | |
| Loan | 1000 | | | |
| Covenant payment | 250 | 250 | 250 | 250 |
| Rec⁻ ᵣᵣed Income Tax | 107 | 107 | 107 | 107 |
| **The charity pays** | | | | |
| Loan repayment | 250 | 250 | 250 | 250 |
| **Total receipts** | 1107 | 107 | 107 | 107 |
| **Cumulative** | 1107 | 1214 | 1321 | 1428 |

* *The date of the loan is normally one day before the first instalment is repaid and the first annual covenant payment is made.*

** *If the donor pays Higher Rate Tax he will be eligible for Higher Rate Relief. The benefits of Higher Rate Relief for a £10 covenant payment are shown in the previous table.*

The tax advantages of a loan-covenant are striking. They make this form of giving much more attractive than a simple donation. A basic rate taxpayer can increase the value of his gift by 42.8%, and for a person paying tax at the highest rate can quadruple the value of a gift at no extra cost to himself. But because of the paper-work involved, in practice it will only be worth using a loan-covenant for a donation of a reasonable size, say £20–£25 or more. For smaller donations the cost of administration would probably exceed any tax advantage that could be enjoyed.

# 4. Conclusions

In comparing the tax situation for legacies, for lifetime gifts of capital and for loan-covenants the following conclusions can be drawn:

1. The most effective way of giving is out of income under Deed of Covenant (and for single donations under a Loan-Covenant agreement). The tax advantage to the charity is 42.8% and the donor may also be eligible for Higher Rate Relief. Wherever possible, people who wish to support a charity should be persuaded to do so during their lifetime under Deed of Covenant. (This does not apply for very large gifts which cannot reasonably be made out of the donor's income.)

2. Where a donor wishes to donate an asset to a charity and it is showing a loss (for Capital Gains Tax), he would do better to sell the asset to the charity and to donate the purchase price. In this way he will be able to establish a loss to offset against any chargeable gains he might make. And the purchase price can be donated under Deed of Covenant, of course.

3. Where a donor has an asset which is showing a substantial capital gain, instead of donating cash to the charity he should donate the asset which he can subsequently re-purchase from the charity. In this way a higher purchase price for Capital Gains Tax purposes can be established, which will reduce the liability to Capital Gains Tax when the asset is eventually sold, but this is never as advantageous as donating the cash under Deed of Covenant (*see 1 above*).

4. Many people only wish to give substantially to charity on their death. Although a legacy to charity is 'neutral' for tax purposes, that is that there is no actual tax that can be recovered, the 'cost' of making a legacy to charity is reduced by the Capital Transfer Tax that would otherwise be payable if the money was bequeathed to a non-exempt beneficiary. With Capital Transfer Tax on death rising up to 75% the advantages of giving a legacy to charity are considerable. These should be fully explained to supporters in order to encourage them to give and to give more substantially to charity in their Will.

# APPENDIX 2

# Provisions for family and dependants

A donor may make a Will disposing of his estate as he pleases. But despite his Will, there are certain dependants for whom provision from his estate can be made, regardless of whether they have been mentioned in the Will or not. The law entitling certain dependants to obtain financial provision from a deceased's estate is set out in the *1975 Inheritance (Provision for Family and Dependants) Act*. This Act applies where the deceased person is domiciled in England or Wales. In Scotland other provisions exist under Scottish law.

Even where a charity is named as a major beneficiary, the Will can be contested by certain members of the deceased's family and other dependants where they feel that they have not been reasonably provided for. So although a person may wish to benefit a charity in his Will, the charity is only *certain* of receiving the money if the testator has also made adequate provision for his dependants.

The following people have a right to make a claim under the 1975 Inheritance Act:

1. The wife or husband of the deceased;
2. A former wife or husband who has not remarried at the time of the deceased's death;
3. A child of the deceased and any other person who as a result of a marriage of the deceased was treated as being a child of the family in relation to that marriage;
4. Any other person who immediately before the death of the deceased was being maintained wholly or partly by the deceased.

Any of these people may apply to the Courts within six months of the death of the deceased for reasonable financial provision to be made for themselves. What is 'reasonable financial provision' is a matter for the Courts to decide; but the following will be taken into account:

(a) The size and nature of the estate of the deceased;

(b) The financial resources and needs of other beneficiaries of the estate;

(c) Any other matter which the Court deems to be relevant (including any physical or mental disability of the applicant, the age of the applicant, (if a spouse) the duration of the marriage, and any contribution made by the applicant in cash or kind towards the welfare of the family of the deceased).

The full details are spelled out in the Act and are elaborated by subsequent case law on the subject. The Court may order that the applicant receive periodic payments from the estate, a lump sum, or a transfer of specific assets from the estate.

Where the deceased has made capital transfers during the last six years of his life so that money is not available from his estate to make provision for any applicant under the 1975 Inheritance Act, and the capital transfers have been made *with the intention of defeating an application for financial provision* under the Act, then the Court has the power under Section 10 of the Act to order the recipient to repay any or all of the money he has received. This applies whether or not the beneficiary holds any interest in the property he has received from the deceased at the time the order is made; but the recipient cannot be asked to repay more than:

(a) The net amount he received, less any Capital Transfer Tax he has paid in respect of the gift.

(b) (If the gift was in kind) the value of the property at the date of the deceased's death (or if the property has been disposed of prior to the deceased's death, the value at the date of disposal) less any Capital Transfer Tax paid by the recipient in respect of the gift.

Before the Court can order the repayment of any gift it has to be satisfied on four counts:

1. That the gift was made to the recipient otherwise than for valuable consideration (this can include sales of assets at below market value).

138

2. That the gift was made within six years of the deceased's death.

3. That the donor had the intention when making the gift of avoiding his financial responsibilities and defeating any application for support from his estate through lack of funds.

4. That the estate of the deceased has insufficient funds to meet the claims of applicants for reasonable financial provision under the 1975 Inheritance Act.

Section 10 was introduced as an anti-avoidance measure. The likelihood of any charity having to repay any money it has already received is not great. Not only do the four conditions mentioned above have to be met, but the gift needs to be reasonably substantial for it to be worth anyone's while to try to get it repaid.

# APPENDIX 3

# Ex-gratia payments by charities

Where a charity is a residuary legatee (or where the residuary estate is to be applied to charitable purposes), the charity will be entitled to receive that part of the residue which it has been bequeathed.

Certain deductions are permitted in calculating the value of the residue:

1. Debts and arrears of tax owed by the testator at the time of death,
2. Funeral expenses (but not the provision of a tombstone),
3. Capital Transfer Tax due on the estate,
4. Pecuniary legacies and specific gifts made by the testator in his Will,
5. Legal and other costs incurred in the administration of the estate.

Any other expenditure is not permitted without the consent of the residuary beneficiaries. Where a charity is a residuary beneficiary, it is not able to give such consent freely. Any funds to which it is entitled are charitable funds and subject to the same trusts as the other funds belonging to it. If a payment is made from these funds which is not applied to its own charitable purposes, then this could be a breach of trust.

However, during the administration of a Will the executors may seek the permission of the beneficiaries to make certain payments from the estate which have not been authorised in the Will. Such requests might be for any of the following:

The provision of a tombstone or other memorial.

Provision for family and dependants. Under the *1975 Inheritance (Provision for Family and Dependants) Act*, certain people may have a right to benefit under a Will and these claims can be settled through the Courts or by agreement with the residuary legatees.

Ex-gratia payments to people who have been of service to the deceased and who have not been provided for in the Will (or where inadequate provision has been made.)

Mementos requested by relations or friends of the deceased.

Repair of bequeathed assets before they are handed over to the legatee.

A charity beneficiary will obviously have to respond to such requests. It will give its consent not only basing its decision on the merits of the individual case but also taking into account certain guidelines issued by the Charity Commission for making ex-gratia payments from charitable funds.

On occasions the request will be for an item of small or negligible resale value as a memento. There should be no difficulty in agreeing to such a request. But where the item has any substantial value, then the guidelines for ex-gratia payments would have to be adhered to. Of course, there is nothing to prevent the purchase of the item in question from the estate.

The Charity Commission guidelines are contained in their leaflet TP7, and are as follows:

1. Until the Judgement of Mr. Justice Cross given in the Chancery Division on 23 May 1969 in the cases of *Re Snowden* and *Re Henderson* it was uncertain whether Charity Trustees could lawfully make voluntary payment out of charity funds in pursuance of a moral obligation, even with the authority of the Court or of the Attorney General. However, in those cases the Judge held that the Court and the Attorney General have a discretionary power to give authority to charity trustees to make ex gratia payments out of funds held on charitable trusts.

2. As to the procedure to be adopted in such cases, the Judge expressed the view that the following was reasonable. In cases where a charity wished to make an ex gratia payment the charity should apply to the Charity Commission or the Department of Education and Science (in the case of an educational charity). Where the funds in question were held on trust for general charitable purposes application should be made to the Treasury Solicitor. The Commissioners or the Department or the Treasury Solicitor (as the case might be) would look into the facts and make a report to the Attorney General, who would decide whether or not to authorise the payment. The Attorney General would normally decide himself whether or not the payment should be authorised but if he was in doubt what

course to take in any particular case he could apply ex parte to the Court for guidance.

3. It will be observed that the Judge was dealing with two types of cases. The first type (*Re Snowden*) concerned gifts to particular charities. If a charity considers that it is under a moral obligation to make a payment out of its entitlement then the charity (and not the persons claiming to be morally entitled to the payment) should apply to the Commissioners or the Department. The Commissioners or the Department will verify the facts on which the application is based (if necessary calling for evidence by statutory declaration or otherwise), and when satisfied as to the facts they will consider whether they could recommend that the charity should be authorised to make payment and if so whether the amount proposed is reasonable. In this connection it should be observed that in the course of his Judgement Mr. Justice Cross, after holding that the Court and the Attorney General had power to authorise ex gratia payments out of charity funds, continued as follows:

"It is, however, a power which is not to be exercised lightly or on slender grounds but only in cases where it can be fairly said that if the charity were an individual it would be morally wrong of him to refuse to make the payment. Without seeking in any way to fetter the discretion of the Attorney General in this field, I would suggest that there may well be a considerable difference between cases, such as those before me today, where it appears that the Testator never intended the charity to receive so large a gift as it did receive, and cases where the Testator intended the charity to receive what it has received but the Testator's relatives consider that he was not morally justified in leaving his money to a charity rather than to them. An honourable man when satisfied that part of a legacy which he has been paid was not intended by the Testator for him at all but for someone else, and that it has only come to him through some oversight or legal technicality, would certainly feel under a moral obligation to hand that part over to the person who was intended to have it. On the other hand, if a Testator in the exercise of his legal right to dispose of his property as he likes chooses to give his estate to A rather than to B the fact that B is bitterly disappointed and considers that the Testator acted very wrongly is not in itself a reason why A should feel under a moral obligation to hand over the estate or any part of it to B. I do not, of course, mean to say that there can never be cases in the second category in which an ex gratia payment out of charity funds would be justified; a case in which it would, perhaps, be justified might be where a Testator in making the gift to a charity was breaking a solemn, though legally unenforceable, promise to leave it to someone else: (*see the case of National Provincial Bank v Moore, reported in The Times 27 April 1967*). But I think that the cases in which an ex gratia payment would be justified would be rarer in the second category than in the first."

4. On completion of their enquiries the Commissioners or the Department will submit a report and recommendation in appropriate cases direct to the Attorney General for his decision.

5. It should be emphasised that this procedure is not appropriate in a case which can be disposed of by the Commissioners or the Department by authorising a settlement or compromise under *Section 23* of the *1960 Charities Act* (which covers action proposed or contemplated in the administration of a charity which is expedient in the interests of the charity – *editor's note*).

6. The second type of case (*Re Henderson*) concerned gifts on trust for general charitable purposes. In these cases as there is no specific charity involved the Commissioners and the Department are not concerned. The approach will probably be received from the person who considers himself morally entitled to receive a payment, or perhaps from personal representatives of the estate from which the gift derives, and it should be made to the Treasury Solicitor. The latter will verify the facts and report to the Attorney General for his decision.

7. In both types of case the Attorney General will notify his decision to the Commissioners or the Department or the Treasury Solicitor, as the case may be, who will inform the applicant of the result of his application.

# APPENDIX 4

# The Smee and Ford notification service

The *Smee and Ford Agency* has been established for well over a hundred years. It supplies a legacy notification service for many charitable organisations, both large and small. Subscribers to the service are notified every time that their charity has been mentioned in a Will.

The service is based solely on an inspection of the public records at Somerset House, which are searched daily for these notifications. Over 5,000 Wills are scanned each week, and of these about 200–250 contain charitable bequests.

There are, broadly speaking, two types of bequest – the 'direct bequest', where a charity is mentioned by name; and the 'discretionary bequest', where money is left for charitable purposes at some nominated person's discretion (usually the executor or trustee of the Will). A subscriber to the *Direct Notification Service* will receive notification only when the charity is specifically mentioned by name.

Just because a charity has been bequeathed a certain sum does not mean that the charity will get that sum. There has to be sufficient funds in the estate to meet all the bequests that are made in the Will in full. The financial information about the value of the estate that is publicly available is very limited. In England and Wales the gross and net figures only are stated in the probate (the difference between these figures are the legal and funeral expenses and debts and any tax owing at the time of death). No figure is given for any Capital Transfer Tax that is payable, this being deductible from the net value of the estate. It is also impossible for anyone scrutinising a Will to put a value on items of property and personal effects that are made as specific bequests. So the net estate adjusted for tax and the value of other bequests (which is the amount available for distribution) cannot be calculated from the publicly available documents.

The position is further aggravated by the legislation passed in 1982 whereby estates of under £25,000 no longer carry accurate gross and net figures, but are merely stated as 'not exceeding £25,000' or 'not exceeding £10,000' (the only two figures used). In the latter case there may be only £5 in the whole estate!

Thus the mere notification that a charity is bequeathed £500, say, under a Will does not necessarily guarantee that such a sum will actually be handed over to that charity. However, in the great majority of cases, estates are sufficiently large to be able to pay all the nominated bequests.

When a charity is left the residue of an estate, it will receive what remains after all other bequests have been satisfied, or a proportion of that residue. In such cases it is impossible to estimate with any degree of accuracy the value of the legacy. However, the residuary legatee is entitled to ask the Executors for a financial statement of the estate in order to be satisfied that the estate has been distributed as the Testator intended, and that it has received the proper share.

Some Wills, while making pecuniary or residuary bequests to charities, make these subject to prior life interests. Very often the spouse or other legatee receives the income from an estate for the rest of their lives, after which the bequests are then made over to the charity. In this case the charity will definitely receive the bequest, but will not know exactly when. The other main condition found in Wills is where bequests are made to charity only if some named beneficiary predeceases the testator, or fails to survive the testator by a stated period. In this case the charity will only receive the bequest if the person concerned does not survive to receive it first; this information cannot be obtained simply by scrutinising the Will.

Occasionally a bequest is stated in ambiguous terms – the most common fault is where the charity is not named properly. In such cases by subscribing to the service a charity can usually ensure that it receives the notification, where it is probably the intended beneficiary, thus giving it a chance to apply for the bequest.

The *Smee and Ford Direct Notification Service* informs each charity when it has been specifically mentioned in a Will. Full details are given of the deceased, the size of the estate, the executors and solicitors dealing with the Will, in addition to information about the bequest itself and any conditions attached to it. This information not only assists charities to predict their legacy income, but in some cases it ensures that they actually receive the sum bequeathed. Direct Notifications are sent for a fee of £1.25 (plus VAT) each, whatever the size of the bequest.

The *Discretionary Notification Service* consists of informing charities of any large bequest (usually £10,000 or more) that is left to charitable bodies or for charitable purposes at the discretion of the executors of the Will or other nominated trustees. The information given is similar to that for the Direct Service. Charities who subscribe to this part of the service receive all general discretionary notifications as well as limited discretionary notifications (where money is left to a particular class of charity, 'charities for old people' or 'cancer research' for instance). The charity is therefore able to write to the Executors or to the solicitors handling the administration of the Will in the hope that they might be considered when the estate is distributed. There can be no guarantee that a charity will succeed in getting money by doing this; but charities do receive income from these appeals, and in some cases quite considerable sums. This *Discretionary Notification Service* is sent on an annual subscription basis – £30 per annum (plus VAT) for 1983. The subscription is payable in advance.

All notifications are posted weekly to every charity. In the case of discretionary notifications particular care is taken to ensure (as far as the vagaries of the Post Office allow) that every client receives their notice at the same time. Accounts are kept as simple as possible and are posted monthly for most of the larger charities, and quarterly (to save overheads for both parties) for the smaller accounts.

For further information about these notification services write to Smee & Ford at The Gallery, 82 The Cut, Waterloo, London SE1 8LW (telephone 01–928 4050).

# APPENDIX 5

# Resources

## 1. The Law

The main law relating to Wills and their administration is contained in the following Acts of Parliament:

**1837 Wills Act** and **1963 Wills Act**

**1925 Administration of Estates Act**, which is the statutory provisions relating to intestacy and the powers of personal representatives

**1965 Administration of Estates (Small Payments) Act**, for small estates where no grant of probate is needed

**1975 Inheritance (Provision for Family and Dependants) Act**, which gives the right to certain persons to claim from an estate.

The following book reviews all aspects of charity law:

**Law Relating to Charities**, by D. G. Cracknell, published by Oyez Longman, £17.50.

## 2. Taxation

The main taxation aspects of legacies and capital transfers are set out in Appendix 1.

For more detailed information in an easily readable form, see:

**The Hambro Tax Guide**, published by Oyez Longman, £8.95

**The Which? Book of Money**, from the Consumers' association, published by Hodder and Stoughton, £9.95

**Covenants: a practical guide**, from the Directory of Social Change, £3.95

For comprehensive coverage of the subject, see:

**Taxation for Executors and Trustees**, by A. R. Mellows, published by Butterworths, £15.00

**Capital Transfer Tax**, by A. L. Chapman, published by TLPC, £12.50.

### 3. Do-it-yourself Wills

For the intrepid amateur who does not mind laughing from the grave as the lawyers grab it all in legal fees, as they try to untangle his ambiguities and cope with his mistakes, the following are two straightforward books aimed at the amateur Will writer:

**Wills and Probate**, from the Consumers' Association, published by Hodder and Stoughton, £3.95

**Write your own Will**, Elliot Right Way Books, 75p

The following is a professionals' handbook which contains model clauses for use in a variety of circumstances:

**The Will Draftsman's Handbook**, Oyez Publishing, £9.95

### 4. Administration of Wills

For personal administrators who are involved in the administration of Wills the following may be useful:

**Wills and Probate**, from the Consumers' Association (see above)

**The Right Way to Prove a Will**, Elliot Right Way Books, 75p

**Probate Practice and Procedure**, Fourmat Publishing, £6.95

### 5. Some useful addresses

**Smee and Ford Notifications Service** (administrative office), Royal Oak House, Oak Street, Fakenham, Norfolk NR21 9DY or (registered office) The Gallery, 82 The Cut, Waterloo, London SE1 8LW

**Probate Personal Application Department**, Principal Registry of the Family Division, 4th Floor, Adelphi Building, John Adam Street, London WC2N 6BB (there are local office registries in Birmingham, Bodmin, Brighton, Bristol, Carlisle, Lincoln, Liverpool, Llandaff, Maidstone, Manchester, Middlesbrough, Newcastle-upon-Tyne, Nottingham, Oxford, Peterborough, Sheffield, Stoke-on-Trent, Winchester, York, and local offices for personal applicants in 94 other locations)

**Inland Revenue Capital Taxes Office**, Minford House, Rockley Road, London W14 for information on the workings of Capital Transfer Tax and Capital Gains Tax.

### 6. Some other fund raising publications

The following fund-raising publications are available from the Directory of Social Change

**Raising Money from Trusts**, £2.95

**Raising Money from Government**, £2.95

**Raising Money from Industry**, £2.95

**Industrial Sponsorship and Joint Promotions**, £2.95

**The Charity Trading Handbook**, £4.95

**A Guide to the Benefits of Charitable Status**, £4.95

**Money and Influence in Europe**, £3.95

All these are available post free from the Directory of Social Change, 9 Mansfield Place, London NW3 1HS.

# Index

# INDEX

# INDEX

*Published simultaneously with this book:*

# LEAVING MONEY TO CHARITY

At present around 95% of people do not leave money to charity in their Will. This represents an important failure by charities to mobilise support for their cause at a time when people should be predisposed to give. But it also represents a challenge.

This new guide is aimed at encouraging people to make charitable bequests. It discusses why they should consider leaving money to charity and shows them how to set about doing so. It covers the following topics:

* Finding out how much you are worth
* Setting about making a Will
* Deciding to leave money to charity
* Choosing a charity to benefit
* Capital Transfer Tax
* The intestacy rules and claims of family and dependants

Charities will find this guide an invaluable aid when approaching their supporters. Written in simple language and set out in an easy-to-read question and answer format, this book will provide the answers to most of the questions that will be asked. For charities wishing to distribute this guide to their supporters, bulk discount terms are available (details on request).

Published by the Directory of Social Change, 9 Mansfield Place, London NW3 1HS.

**Price £1.95**                                 **ISBN 0 907164 12 9**